# ANGOLA IN FERMENT

# ANGOLA IN FERMENT

*The Background and Prospects*

*of Angolan Nationalism*

*By*

THOMAS OKUMA

*Beacon Press   Boston*

Published simultaneously in Canada by
S. J. Reginald Saunders and Co., Ltd., Toronto

*Library of Congress catalog card number:* 62–7896

Printed in the United States of America

# ACKNOWLEDGMENTS

This book, based upon my years in Angola, was made possible through the cooperation of my colleagues in arranging a fellowship grant. I have been much helped by the African Studies Program of Boston University, especially by Dr. Ruth Schachter, who has given much of her time to read and criticize the manuscript. I am indebted to Professor Rupert Emerson for his foreword and to Professor James Duffy for his editorial assistance. A special word of gratitude is due to my wife, who encouraged me to write the book. There are many others not mentioned, here and abroad, who have also been of great help. I am deeply grateful to them.

8136

# FOREWORD

While the great tides of African destiny sweep forward, Portugal clings with forlorn but stubborn pride to the hopes and illusions of a bygone age. The memory that Portugal was the first of the European powers to explore the African coast and establish posts on African soil was recently brought to new life by the celebration of the fifth centenary of the death of Henry the Navigator, a celebration deliberately aimed to dramatize the country's world mission. It has been the dream of the Portuguese that they might be, not the last of the powers to leave Africa, but the only one which would fuse its African, Asian and European peoples into a single national whole, perhaps even—wistfully—bringing multiracial Brazil back into the fold.

Whether or not there are actually differences of substance between them, the Portuguese are firm in the belief that they are not to be put in the same basket as the other colonial powers in Africa and that their motives and goals are not only different but also purer and more closely akin to the Christian ideal. Mr. Okuma has caught the flavor of their view in citing the Portuguese as seeing their colonization as "a transcendent campaign, a sharing of spiritual values." The standard French belief in the doctrine of assimilation as the proper end of colonialism is often no more than a pale shadow of the persuasion of the Portuguese that their mission is to bring the light, as they see it, to those who live in darkness. With both pained and amused superiority they have watched the British and French abandon their African holdings. As the Portuguese saw it, the Belgians in the Congo, Angola's neighbors to the north, were upstart newcomers to Africa who failed to identify themselves with the Africans and therefore fled as soon as trouble broke out. The Portuguese have been in Angola half a millennium and plan to stay.

The more sober and worldly-wise among them have, of course, known that the winds which blow through Africa must in due course penetrate to them as well, but the conviction of Portugal's difference from the others dies hard. The sense of a distinctive mission is deep ingrained and makes all the more intolerable, if not impossible, the need to face up to the fact that much of Angola is in revolt, that Portuguese Guinea has had the first signals of attack, and that Mozambique's day of reckoning cannot be far off.

Even more than other colonizers, the Portuguese have had a profound sense that their overseas subjects, their potential fellow citizens, really love them and yearn to enter into the Portuguese soul and way of life. The counterpart of this proposition is, of course, the characteristic colonial conviction that all disaffection and disturbance come from alien influences which seek to disrupt the tranquil harmony of the far-flung Portuguese community. In the same fashion the critics of Portugal's role and policy in Africa are either evil in intent or unaware of the inward reality.

From this sense of the difference between the Portuguese position and that of other colonizers, as well as from the more mundane desire to evade prying eyes, springs Portugal's outrageous insistence that her overseas possessions do not fall in the category of nonself-governing territories on which reports must be rendered to the United Nations under Chapter XI of the Charter. If a mere declaration by a colonial power that its dependencies are not dependent could turn the trick, then Chapter XI would have lost all force. That the people of Portugal are themselves not democratically self-governing at home does not change the fact that the peoples of Angola and Mozambique "have not yet attained a full measure of self-government," as the Charter puts it. Indeed, it would be hard to find any African territory which has a lesser measure of self-government than the Portuguese colonies.

The Portuguese position can be challenged at either or both of two levels: either in its basic presumption that the ideal goal is a mixed society lacking consciousness of color in which all are equally assimilated to a common European model, or in terms of the successes and failures in moving toward that goal.

On the first score, one is involved immediately in a debate as to ultimate values which will presumably be carried on throughout eternity. The ideal which the Portuguese have set for themselves is certainly not one to be dismissed out of hand. It must be acknowledged to have a grandeur of its own even though it may be attacked, not only on the lesser ground of feasibility but also on the higher ground of questioning the right of any culture to set itself up as the model to which alien societies must conform. In a period when *négritude* and the African Personality are commanding heights on the African landscape, it is not to be expected that the Portuguese formula will win much favor.

On the second score the grounds of challenge are clearer, since what is involved is an objective evaluation of what has and has not been done for the mass of the Africans on whom Portuguese rule has been imposed. Here, as Mr. Okuma demonstrates in detail, the five hundred years of Portuguese association with Angola begin to turn against the occupier, even though it be conceded at the outset that for only a fraction of the time was there effective occupation of any substantial portion of the country. If this half-millennium is a key part of the Portuguese title deeds to its African territory, it must also be brought into the accounting as to what has been done. Five hundred years is a long time in which to have accomplished so shockingly little. The Portuguese achievement will not stand comparison with what the other colonial powers have succeeded in doing in a far shorter time. Illiteracy, poverty and complete subjection to alien rule are the end result of Portugal's centuries of colonial rule in Angola for the overwhelming majority of the Africans.

It is not infrequently the boast of the Portuguese that they have imposed no color but only a culture bar; and it undoubtedly stands to their credit that the color of a man's skin is not regarded as the determinant of his place in the social order. The contrast between the kind of society which has been brought into being in Angola and Mozambique as compared with Southern Rhodesia and South Africa is real and welcome; but it is a major offset to the relatively free and easy race relationships that the large-scale economic development of the latter countries has little in the way of a counterpart in the former.

Nor is the ease in race relationships as all-embracing or as enduring a matter as an ideal statement of it might make it out to be. To one coming to Angola from Senegal, Ghana and Nigeria, as I did in December 1960, it is a painful experience to observe the difference in bearing and attitude of the Africans in these countries as contrasted with the Africans of Angola. If the masses in both areas are still living close to the bottom level of poverty, the West Africans *d'expression française et anglaise,* as the current phrase has it, somehow bear their poverty with a good cheer and hopefulness which is strikingly absent among the browbeaten Africans of Angola. Where the former bubble over with a sense of friendliness, vitality and eager self-confidence in a world which is coming into their own grasp, the Angolan Africans, in my limited contact with them in Luanda and the countryside, conveyed a sense of sullen resentment of the inferior and servile position which has been forced upon them. It may be that a handful of Africans in the upper reaches of Angolan society have come to full and casual acceptance among the ruling Portuguese; in the lower reaches the Africans in their millions have remained "natives," officially labeled "uncivilized" and subject to discriminatory administrative and judicial treatment, at least until the grant of formal legal equality in August 1961. Those employed by whites were exposed to arbitrary punishment and to discipline by the police.

One aspect of the situation which has attracted much international comment over the past decades and which has undoubtedly played a significant role in stimulating the present revolt is the labor question. Although the Portuguese authorities and apologists have vehemently denied the continued existence of forced labor, much evidence has been piled up to indicate that one or another form of compulsion has in fact been widely utilized to produce a labor supply for both government and private employers. Whether it be viewed as an impairment of Portuguese spiritual pretensions or as an appropriate elaboration of them, much emphasis has habitually been laid by the Portuguese on the "dignity of labor." The official machineries, operating at the bottom through the chiefs and village headmen, have been available to make sure that the Africans did not miss their opportunity to share in this dignity.

A tragic feature of the recent past is that the admirable absence of racial feeling among the Portuguese has tended to give way to a new sense of suspicion and hostility between the races. Leaving aside the special pressures generated by the upheavals which started in Luanda in February 1961, the key element working in this direction has presumably been the Lisbon-sponsored effort to introduce a large number of Portuguese settlers into Angola. This has had the double purpose of easing the pressure of the poverty-stricken masses in Portugal itself and of amplifying the Portuguese presence in Africa.

The importation of tens of thousands of Portuguese into Angola was intended to have a number of beneficial effects, but it has also done much damage. On the good side of the ledger, from the Portuguese standpoint, was the expectation that Portugal's claim to and actual hold upon the country would be established beyond challenge if enough Portuguese settled there. It was further hoped that the European newcomers would both directly bring about a speedier development of the economy and serve as guides and instructors for the Africans among whom they would be living. A number of Portuguese peasants and middle-sized farmers have been settled on the land in planned colonization schemes and have demonstrated the possibility of successful European farming under Angolan conditions.

The most dangerous feature of the Portuguese incursion has been the lowering of the ceiling for African employment precisely at the time when African political consciousness was being roused and an increasing number of Africans were looking for employment in the modern sector of the economy. Many of the Portuguese who came to Angola were unskilled and unready to settle on the farms which were being opened up. In consequence they drifted into the cities and towns and cut in on the lower-level and intermediate jobs to which the Africans aspired and which in some instances they had already occupied. As a result of the pressure of the newcomers not only clerical jobs but also such employment as waiters, taxi drivers and filling station attendants tended to be taken over by whites to the exclusion of the Africans, and small stores run by whites multiplied in African sections of the towns. As an African in Luanda scornfully put it to me: Portuguese men were even wandering the streets of the city trying to peddle lottery tickets. Economic development was advancing far too slowly to absorb both the rising Africans and the Europeans who were coming into the labor market.

A monster with two evil heads was the inevitable result. One head was the growth of a sense of frustration and bitterness on the part of the Africans who found themselves pressed down to even lower economic levels than they had occupied before. In addition they saw substantial quantities of land, to which they would undoubtedly at some point lay claim, vanishing into European hands.

The other head was the spread among the Europeans of a sense that the white man's position and prerogatives must be protected against the threatened encroachments of the blacks. In Angola as elsewhere in the world it has been the lower ranges of the white community—the ranges which come most directly into competition with the Africans—which have felt most rancorously the need to close the white ranks and keep the black man where he belongs. As a trivial example, I have myself seen the feud which developed in one household between an illiterate immigrant Portuguese maid and a somewhat more educated Angolan house "boy." As far as an outsider could determine, it was wholly the Portuguese woman who picked the fight, essentially on the grounds that she had a special dignity and status which must be preserved against African intrusion. Africans, she contended, should be beaten to teach them their place.

It is to the multiplication of such feuds and their expansion to represent the outlook of entire communities that one must turn for an understanding of some of the most shocking episodes and aspects of the Angolan rising and its repression. Atrocities have been committed by both sides, but, if the reports are to be believed, peculiar savagery attended the indiscriminate attack by whites on Africans in Luanda and many other places. In fact the entire Portuguese campaign appears to have been conducted with ruthless severity, killing many thousands of Africans and driving tens of thousands across the border to take refuge in the Congo. *The Observer* of London commented on June 4, 1961, that in the past month the Portuguese had killed more Africans in Angola than had been killed in the Union of South Africa during the last hundred years—and it feared that the worst was yet to come.

By an ironic twist of fate the revolt in Angola has driven the

Portuguese close to the point of acting in flat contradiction to the principles which have been their proudest boast. Recognizing that their bitterest and most dangerous enemies are the people who have achieved or made an approach to assimilation—the "civilized" as contrasted with the "noncivilized"—the Portuguese have, according to a number of accounts, attempted to remove from circulation by imprisonment or other means all Africans who demonstrate any outward evidence of contact with the modern world. Teachers, religious leaders, literates, possessors of books, radios or bicycles—these are the suspect characters against whom the colonial regime has swung into action in an effort to check the revolt before it picks up so great momentum as to be wholly beyond control.

Setting off from these premises one may state the dilemma which confronts the Portuguese in something like the following terms. It is their claim to be devoted to the task of bringing civilization to the Africans over whom they have asserted their rule in the course of the centuries. In part because of their lack of race feeling they regard themselves as uniquely qualified for this mission of assimilation which they have been performing and which they must still project far into the future. But in order to maintain their hold in Africa they must keep education for Africans and other modernizing influences at a minimum; otherwise they will find their best pupils the leaders of the nationalists who oppose them. To prevent revolt they must closely supervise every one with any education or with any economic or social status of a Western type, and, if trouble threatens, Africans who fall in the preceding category should be rounded up and isolated. Thus, in order to carry on the work of civilization that is Portugal's special mission it is necessary to guard the Africans against education and advancement and to view with suspicion all those who show any interest in the modern world or who threaten to succumb to that most dangerous of diseases: thinking for themselves. Because those who think for themselves might come to the point of acting for themselves as well.

Translated into terms of practical international politics this dilemma takes the shape of a close relationship between Portugal and South Africa. Certainly no other state in Africa and perhaps no other state in the world at large, could take as sympathetic a

view of Portugal. Thus a strange intimacy and possibly a defensive
alliance link the champion of *apartheid* and white supremacy with
the champion of assimilation and racial equality.

In creating a dilemma for themselves in Angola, the Portuguese have also created a major dilemma or two for the rest of the
world. The heart of the matter is the question as to how the
Angolan—and prospectively the Mozambique—issue is to be dealt
with from here on out. It is a question which is very simple to
ask and extraordinarily hard to answer.

We have little reason to doubt that in the relatively near
future Angola will either achieve independence or be irresistibly
moving toward it in the pattern which has been established by so
many of the former colonies. There is, however, equally little
reason to doubt that Angola's Africans are not ready to assume responsibility for the management of a state which must take its place
in the modern world. In greater or less degree all the African
states and the remaining European dependencies which will soon
come to independence are lamentably short of trained and experienced manpower, but none has approached independence as desti-
tute of training and experience as Angola. Even the neighboring
Congo, for all the grievous shortcomings of the Belgians, had a
broad-based educational system, had drawn a large number of Africans into middle-level employments of many descriptions, and had
developed various of the ingredients of a high-powered modern
economy. Given the failure of the Portuguese to educate the mass
of the Africans, to develop the economy and to lead the Africans
forward into self-government, it would be a miracle if Angola were
now in a position to take over the running of its own affairs without massive external aid. Lisbon's answer is, of course, to insist that
Angola be left a part of the national domain in order that the
Portuguese may complete the work which they began so long ago.
On two counts this answer must be rejected. The Portuguese record
gives scant support to the notion that they either will or can do
the kind of a job which is already long overdue; and even if there
were unmistakable indication of a change of heart and mind, it is
wholly likely that the Angolan nationalists would reject Portuguese
collaboration, particularly after the experience of the last few
months.

If Portugal is rejected, where else can the Angolans turn? The most desirable answer is that Angola should move ahead toward independence under the aegis of the United Nations. A very strong case can be made for the proposition that the ideal solution would be a trusteeship administered by the United Nations itself, a possibility under the charter which has been proposed in several instances but never yet attempted. In theory such a step would remove Angola from the rivalry of the powers by placing the country under international auspices and open to it the doors for international aid while it prepared itself for full independence in, say, five or ten years time.

Theory and practice, however, are likely to be very far apart. Far from being above the jealousies and conflicts of the powers, the United Nations habitually runs the risk of being trapped in the evil web they have spun. In the Congo it has been able to make signal contributions in an extraordinarily difficult situation, but precisely the Congo experience, which has brought so much bad feeling and bitter recrimination within UN, may preclude any similar activity elsewhere. Furthermore, it is probable that the African states, no doubt backed by the Communist bloc and a number of the Asian countries, would repudiate any solution which denied the ability of an African people to govern itself and which involved the introduction of alien (i.e., non-African) elements of control into the government of an African country.

We can be sure of only one thing: that we shall hear much more of Angola before it comes to a definitive turning of the ways. In the interval, this book gives the background and the facts on the basis of which intelligent decisions can be made.

RUPERT EMERSON

*Harvard University,*
*September 1961*

# CONTENTS

# TABLES

Portugal is in Africa and Portugal will remain in Africa.
—*Dr. Castro Fernandez*

All that we care for is to have our own land. . . . We do not wish to have the country of Portugal joined to ours any longer.
—*African Angolan Nationalist*

# INTRODUCTION

Four major incidents in the two-year period 1959-1961 shattered the five centuries of relative peaceful coexistence between Africans and the Portuguese in Angola.

The first of these incidents was the series of disturbances in the Portuguese Congo which resulted from the January 1959 riots in Leopoldville, capital of the Belgian Congo. Africans in the lower Congo saw Abako, the political party of the Bakongos, as the instrument to restore the Congo kingdom. Portuguese authorities arrested and punished many Africans of the Bakongo tribe, especially in the district of São Salvador, the ancient site of the Bakongo kingdom.

The second incident was the announcement by the government in March 1959 of the names of forty Africans who were guilty of "actions against the State." Twelve of the forty resided outside Angola; the other twenty-eight Africans were arrested and imprisoned.

The third occurred in July 1960, in the village of Catete, 34 miles from Luanda. The occasion was the arrest and deportation of one of their "sons," Dr. Agostinho Neto. The people of Catete marched *en masse* to the administration to protest the action taken by the police. The administrator made a hurried call to the governor-general in Luanda, and the authorities dispatched a military police unit to Catete. The clash between the villagers and the police resulted in the death of thirty-eight persons.

The fourth incident took place in Luanda. Reports coming from Angola on the riots that broke out during the weekend of February 5, 1961, were confused. Officials said that a group of Africans attacked and killed four European policemen. Others attacked the midtown military prison and a police station near the *Museque*, the African section of the city. Further shooting at the

1

funeral services of the slain European policemen added to the total
killed and wounded. When the count was made, thirty-one were
dead, fifty-three were wounded and over one hundred Africans were
arrested.[1]

These disturbances raise the question: Is Angola to become
another Congo? The answer lies in how the Portuguese meet the
present situation. So far their actions have indicated a lack of understanding.

The Portuguese have a simple answer to explain these sudden
outbursts of violence. They say Communists are the cause of these
disturbances. Governor-General Alvaro da Silva Tavares, explaining
the February 5 Luanda riots, said it was all the work of Communist
agitators. He added that the attacks had been organized abroad.
Salazar's spokesmen in Lisbon said the guns used were made in
Czechoslovakia, which proved to the Portuguese that outside agents
had provoked the uprisings.[2] If the Portuguese continue to hold the
belief that Communists are causing these disturbances, there is real
danger that Angola will become another Congo.

The clash in Angola is between two nationalisms: Portuguese
on the one hand, and African on the other. The unyielding positions
of the two antagonists will force nations to choose sides. Portugal, as
a member of NATO, will appeal to her Western allies for support.
Angolan nationalist groups will seek aid from the Afro-Asian groups
and the Communist bloc. Angola can become another battleground
for the "cold war."

Portuguese nationalism is based upon the belief that Portugal
will continue to be in authority in Angola for another five centuries.
The disturbances in the Portuguese Congo, the arrest of the twenty-
eight African nationalist leaders, the protest by the villagers at Catete,
the uprisings in Luanda—all these incidents challenge this assump-
tion. Opposition to the Portuguese, however, did not crop up over-
night. The seeds of modern nationalism were sown with the arrival
of the European colonial powers in Africa. The coming of Europeans
set forth a chain of events: the challenge of Western ideas and
technology to tribal ways, and the decline of the traditional ruling
groups, whose status was usually inherited. This created a new
polarity within the social structure, in which the doctor challenged
the witch doctor, the modernists belittled the traditionalists, and the

literates gained power over the illiterates. Europeans assumed the military, police, political, religious and judicial functions which were the traditional priorities of the chief.

My concern in this book is to examine these forces which gave birth to nationalist movements in Angola. By "nationalist" I mean, in the words of Thomas Hodgkin, "any organization or group that explicitly asserts the rights, claims, and aspirations of a given society in opposition to European authority, whatever its institutional form and objectives." [3] I do not restrict the term "nationalism," as James Coleman does, "to describe only those types of organizations which are essentially political, not religious, economic or educational, in character, and which have as their object the realization of self-government or independence for a recognizable African nation or nation to be." [4] Coleman's restrictive definition of "nationalism" would seem to imply that nationalism does not exist in Angola. Political parties do not exist in Angola, but this is because they are illegal; nationalism is real in Angola. Hodgkin terms it " 'incipient nationalism' as contrasted with the 'developed nationalism' of say, the Gold Coast." [5] The reality of "incipient nationalism" makes this study exploratory, since the nationalist movement is still developing in Angola. The stages of this development will depend upon the policies pursued by the Portuguese in governing their territories.

My first chapter describes the setting; the second chapter discusses Portuguese colonial policies. Succeeding chapters examine the disruptive forces of the West, the rise of Angolan nationalist movements, the attacks upon Portugal in the United Nations by the Afro-Asian groups, and the alliance of the United States with Portugal. The study will conclude with speculations about the future of Angola.

Documentary materials for such a study as this are very limited. Sources on the pre-European history of Angolan tribes are virtually nonexistent. All forms of present day communication in Angola—press, radio, books, pamphlets—are rigorously censored by the Portuguese government. In writing this book I have, therefore, relied upon the personal knowledge and observations gained during almost a decade of residence, research and missionary work in Portuguese Angola. But since this book is intended to be a concise and objective study, encompassing only the most relevant, important and ascertainable facts, I have utilized my personal knowledge only after examining and citing all available and reliable documents, records and statistics. Though I have lived in Angola for many years, I must say that Africans in Angola are reluctant to provide information to outsiders. There is always the danger that such conversations may be interpreted by the police—PIDE (*Policia Internacional de Defesa do Estado*)—as "actions against the State."

It is important to bear in mind, incidentally, that statistical figures may change through the years, but the basic relationship between the home country and her overseas territories remains the same.

My hope is that this book will help the reader to understand the nature of the rapid changes taking place in Angola.

# I. THE SETTING

## The Name, the Land, Its Resources

Angola is named after the ancient dynasty of Ngola, chief of the Kimbundu people in the Dongo region. The boundaries of Ngola's kingdom were not certain. An estimate would be "the country lying between the Dande River in the North and the Cuanza in the South and extending from the coast back into the Dongo as far as the modern city of Malange, although some scholars project the eastern boundaries all the way to the Congo River." [1]

The land area of the present Angola extends beyond the original kingdom of Ngola. The present boundaries are: the Republic of Congo to the north; the Republic of Congo and Northern Rhodesia in the east; and South-West Africa in the south. Angola is roughly rectangular in shape, covering an area of 481,351 square miles. This is approximately twice the size of Texas; over fourteen times the area of Portugal; and a little more than half the size of Angola's northern neighbor, the Republic of Congo. Her coastline stretches for about 1,000 miles from the Congo River to the Cunene River on the borders of South-West Africa. Her chief ports are Luanda and Lobito.

The distinguishing topographical feature of Angola is a vast plateau rising to a height of over 6,000 feet from an abrupt incline 150 miles inland from the Atlantic coast. Climatic conditions vary with the corresponding altitudes. In general, the coastal areas are hot and humid during the months of January through March; pleasantly comfortable May through September. The climate on the plateau is agreeable and healthful. The coldest months are June and July, with temperatures reaching 32 degrees Fahrenheit and often much lower. The seasons are divided into dry and wet. The dry

5

season lasts from May through September, with an occasional thundershower toward the end of August. The wet months run from October through the middle of May, with a short dry spell of three or four weeks in January or February. The average rainfall during these wet months, recorded for 1941-1950 in Nova Lisboa, was 55.51 inches.

Dr. David Santos, director of the Luanda Meteorological Observatory, classifies the climatic conditions of Angola as: "Wet, tropical climate in the north, from Cabinda to Ambriz; wet, moderate, tropical climate, in the region which begins a little to the north of Luanda and ends at Moçamedes (Mossâmedes) in the region of Malange and in the east zone; wet, severe climate in the south of Moçamedes; dry, mild climate in the central and south plateaus; desert climate in the south zone between the plateau and the South-West African frontier." [2]

Turning from climate to economy, we can note that Angola is primarily an agricultural country, a fact clearly reflected in statistics on Angola's recent exports. In recent years, 75 per cent of the total tonnage of exported products has consisted of agricultural products, chiefly coffee, sisal, corn, fish meal, cotton, sugar, rice, palm kernels, beans, dry manioc, palm oil, and wood and timber. Coffee alone accounts for 49 per cent of the tonnage of exported agricultural products. Fifteen per cent of the total tonnage of exported products has consisted of minerals, chiefly copper, diamonds, manganese ore, iron ore, and salt. The chief mineral export has been diamonds (743,930 carats in 1956 [3]). Monetary values are more economically meaningful than tons; and the Angolan monetary unit, the Portuguese escudo, currently is equivalent to 3½ U.S. cents. Expressed in terms of this current ratio of monetary values, Angola exported in 1959: $48,545,000 worth of coffee; $20,860,000 of diamonds; $9,150,000 of sisal; $7,525,000 of corn; $7,175,000 of fish meal; $3,640,000 of cotton; $3,465,000 of iron ore; and $2,695,000 of sugar.

Industrialization has been slow in Angola, partly because of the lack of two principal raw materials: iron and coal. The discovery of oil in the outskirts of Luanda and the explorations now being conducted in Cabinda on the enclave of the Congo River may speed the pace of Angolan industrialization. Open-pit mining of iron ore in the Bailundu mountains may also contribute to a faster rate of industrial growth. The firm of Krupp's, in Essen, Germany, has just made a loan of some $42,000,000 to the Companhia Mineira do Lobito to help in the development of these mineral resources. The lack of capital, inadequate modern transport facilities from the mining areas to the railroad, and the scarcity of skilled industrial workers are stumbling blocks to further development of the Angolan economy.

Cheap water power for industrial development is abundant. Three large hydroelectric plants have been constructed. The Mabubas plant, located 45 miles from Luanda, supplies that city with light and power for small industries. Biopio, situated 22 miles from the mouth of the Catumbela River, supplies electricity to the towns of Benguela and Lobito. Matala, utilizing the waters of the Cunene River, located in the Huila district, furnishes electricity to Sá da Bandeira and other small towns and villages as well as to the *Colonato de Baixa Cunene*.

## The People

The mining of minerals, explorations for oil, and the development of modern transport systems and cheap water power, all increased tremendously in the years after World War II. But the greatest changes have occurred in the population of Angola. Table I graphically portrays the increase.

I. POPULATIONS OF ANGOLA SINCE 1900 (1956 STATISTICS)[4]

|           | 1900      | 1910      | 1920      | 1940      | 1950      | 1955      |
|-----------|-----------|-----------|-----------|-----------|-----------|-----------|
| Europeans | 9,000     | 12,000    | 20,700    | 44,083    | 78,826    | 109,568   |
| Mestiços  | 7,000     | 9,500     | 10,500    | 28,035    | 29,648    | 30,453    |
| Africans  | 2,700,000 | 2,900,000 | 3,100,000 | 3,665,829 | 4,036,687 | 4,222,117 |
| Others    |           |           |           |           | 105       | 126       |
| Total     | 2,716,000 | 2,921,500 | 3,131,200 | 3,738,010 | 4,145,266 | 4,362,264 |

The striking feature in this table is the phenomenal growth in the European population. In 1955, Angola's total population was 4,362,264; of these, 109,568 were whites. Increased European im-

migration during the five-year period, 1955-1960, raised that figure
to nearly 175,000 in 1961. Portuguese immigrants at the rate of over
1,000 a month arrived in Angola during those years. However, in
1960, more Portuguese left the colony than entered it.

The majority of the population, however, continue to be Africans. Who are the African peoples living in Angola? Are they
related to the peoples of the north, the south or the east? Most
groups now in Angola arrived there in the migrations from the
eastern highlands between A.D. 1450 and 1600. They lived by
plundering the lands and belongings of the aboriginal tribes. Dr.
Merlin W. Ennis, who has studied the pre-European history of the
Ovimbundu people, believes that the migratory groups turned south
when they reached the neighborhood of Lake Chad and crossed the
Congo River. Some of them pushed into the Lunda country and
others came down through Angola. Portuguese writers refer to them
as "Jagas." 5

All tribal groups, however, have their own legends to explain
the coming of their forefathers. Ndulu, one of the Ovimbundu
kingdoms in central Angola, traces the beginning of its dynasty to
the person of Katekula-Mengo, an elephant hunter. Katekula-Mengo
and his wife, Ukungu, came from the northern region and followed
the elephant herds down the course of the Cuanza River. Evidence
of Katekula-Mengo's journey is found in the imprints of his bow and
of Ukungu's basket in the soft rocks of Pungu-a-Ndongo.

The reason the migrants left their northern homeland is a
matter of conjecture. Dr. Gladwyn Childs offers the hypothesis that
"its immediate cause may have been the prolonged wars between the
Portuguese and Ngola which ended in 1671. . . . The highlands
of Ndulu (Andulu) offered a remote and peaceful refuge." 6

Each migratory group produced its own political and social
structures. The differences, however, varied but slightly among the
tribal groups. For purposes of comparison, let us examine two—the
Ndongo and the Bailundu.

The Ndongo (also called Jinga or Ngola) who now live about
50 to 100 miles north of Malange, are one of the thirteen tribes con-
stituting the Kimbundu-speaking peoples. The tribe was formerly
ruled by a king (titled *Rei Jinga*) who lived in the royal village
(*Mbanza*). A queen, however, might hold the position as head of

the tribe. Dona Ana Sousa, famous in history for her dealings with the Portuguese, was one of the queens. Subordinate to the king were four chieftains (*enexi*). In time of war these served as commanders. Under these divisional chieftains were headmen or village chiefs (*soba*). Each chief was helped by councillors in ruling his village. Succession to the chieftainship was matrilineal. The deceased king's eldest sister's sons were first in the line of succession. If none of the nephews were acceptable to the four chieftains, the king's brother was next in line.

Social practices were in accordance with rank. A commoner, upon approaching the king or chief, fell on his knees, kissed the ground and clapped his hands. Houses were also built according to social position within the tribal pattern. For example, the king lived in a house with two doors and windows. His subordinates were allowed two doors but no windows. Commoners lived in a house with only one door. The king and his chieftains traveled in hammocks. Personal services were rendered to the rulers by their subjects. A commoner was expected to work a day a week for the village chief.[7]

The political and social structure of the Bailundu tribe in central Angola was not too different from that of the Ndongo group. It too was based upon family patterns and royalty. In his study of Umbundu kinship and character, Dr. Childs describes the king of this Bailundu people as a "divine representative and a divine incarnation, but the mode of his succession reveals that he was also a democratically chosen leader. Royal succession was in the male line, sometimes from father to son, but more often from elder to younger brother, to brother's son, or to one even more distantly related. The election is made by the councillors."[8]

Three principal functions of the Bailundu royal household were noted by Dr. Childs. First was the religious function. Ancestral worship was the common practice and the king embodied the spirits of this ancestor worship. Sacrifices were offered at the royal shrine in order: "(a) to ensure a sufficient supply of rain and avoid the dangers caused by hail and lightning; (b) to ensure fertility in all spheres of life; (c) to bring success in hunting. Second, a secular political function. The king represented his nation in dealings with other tribes including the negotiating of trade agreements and the making of warfare on other peoples for purposes of plunder and booty. Third, a judicial function. The king sat as the judge of the highest court of the tribe. Though his decisions were final, the king was 'not only bound by the customs of the tribe, but by the desires of his councillors.' " [9]

Each of the Ovimbundu kings ruled over a number of sub-tribes, and each of these units—composed of from only three to as many as three hundred villages—in turn was governed by a chief. The chieftains were responsible for sending annual tributes to the king. Politically, the village was the local unit. Each village was governed by a headman or elder who represented the village in all aspects of life. "He was responsible for his village to the sub-chief, and through him to the king." [10]

## Portuguese Occupation

European contact with the migratory groups of Angola began before Columbus discovered America. In 1483, Diogo Cão sailed up the Congo River and sent ambassadors to the king of Congo in the name of King John II of Portugal. He returned in 1484 to 1485; in 1491, King John II sent an expedition with a specially appointed embassy and a mission of ten Franciscan friars.[11]

Portuguese penetration into Angola was not easy. In 1592 the Portuguese could claim the beginnings of a colonial government in Luanda, but the Dutch invasion of that city in 1641 brought a halt to Portuguese expansion. Seven years later an armada from Brazil, under the command of Salvador Correia de Sá, attacked the Dutch forces in Luanda. The Portuguese assault on the fortress was unsuccessful, but later the Dutch commander agreed to surrender the town. Salvador Correia de Sá restored order and punished the African chiefs who had transferred their oaths of loyalty to the Dutch during their short period of occupation. The next fifty years brought prosperity to some residents of Angola, especially to those in the slave trade.

In the early 1700s Luanda was known as one of the leading cities on the west coast of Africa. Francisco de Sousa Coutinho, as governor, introduced a program, in 1765, for colonizing Angola. His immediate successors, however, failed to carry on the program he had initiated. In the early 1800s the first Liberal governments of Portugal proposed further reforms. During those years of conquest and reform, the Portuguese concentrated their efforts upon the occupation of the coastal region, Luanda and Benguela. When the Portuguese attempted to occupy the interior, difficulties multiplied a hundredfold. Climatic condition, tropical diseases and lack of communications hindered their campaigns of conquest. The greatest obstacle of all, however, was African tribal resistance. Three military campaigns of the early 1900s were of special note: the Bailundu campaigns of 1902, the Cuanhama massacre of 1904, and the Dembos occupation of 1907.

The 1902 Bailundu campaigns involved the thirteen independent Ovimbundu kingdoms of the Umbundu-speaking groups who lived in the plateau of the Benguela highlands in central Angola. Portuguese attempts to occupy this area inhabited by Ovimbundu (Bailundu peoples) had long been sporadic. During the eighteenth century the Africans of Bailundu caused serious disruptions to the commerce of Benguela, Catumbela, Pungo, Andongo, and Cambambe. The acts of insubordination reached such importance that in 1767 the chief government official of Benguela, José Vierra de Araujo, requested military aid from Captain Sousa Coutinho of Luanda. The captain replied that his men were not yet ready for combat. There were further acts of insurrection against the Portuguese traders and authorities.

On July 11, 1773, the governor of Luanda, D. António de Lencastre, ordered three columns of troops to put down the rebellious Africans living on the Benguela *planoalto*; one, under the command of Lieutenant Manuel Bernardo Pires de Oliveira, headed for Novo Redondo; another, under Captain Albano Caldes de Araujo's command, went by sea to Benguela, with Caconda as their destination; and another left by land on July 16 for Bailundu, under the command of Captain António José da Costa. The troops of Costa met heavy opposition from the Bailundu people. But for a timely arrival of reinforcements from Benguela, Costa's troops would have been defeated. The war ended in 1775.

Government authorities did not generally interfere with inter-

nal tribal warfare. On the contrary, the government often encouraged it. In 1853, with official permission, warriors from the kingdoms of Bailundu and Huambu raided their neighbors in the Seles
region and divided the spoils among themselves. The Seles people
were causing trouble among the European settlers, and the governor
of Benguela, Coelho do Amaral, had no other recourse than to exploit the "inherent and lamentable war-like tendencies of the natives." [12]

Of all the rulers during the last quarter of the nineteenth century, Europeans list Ekuikui II (1876-1893) as the best-remembered
king of the Umbundu kingdom. Early travelers report that Ekuikui's
boundaries measured in circumference the distance of a sixteen days'
march. However, the strategic location of the Bailundu kingdom
was of far more importance than its size. King Ekuikui controlled
the commercial route from the coast to the interior. The king could
effectively seal the country from any invasion by ordering his people to plunder any caravans passing through Bailundu. The incident
of the gift of thirty-five ivories in 1886, as recorded by one of the
early Protestant missionaries, illustrates this point:

> Some time ago the king of Galanganja sent out thirty ivories, some
> of which were for Honjo and some for the king of Bailundu, but the
> king of Bié appropriated them to his own use on the pleas that many
> of his people die in the interior, and he must take his pay when he can
> get it. King Ekuikui sent up Chikulo to remonstrate when his lordship
> of Bié saw fit to add insult to injury by calling the king of Bailundu a
> good-for-nothing heathen, and refusing to entertain his messenger or to
> give him an audience in a regular council. The ivory had already started
> for the coast, so Chikulo made haste to return to Bailundu, reaching
> home the day before the caravan was expected here in camp. The king
> was, of course, highly incensed, and sent out word to have the people
> plunder the caravan. Of course everybody was on hand for that purpose.
> This morning, February 25, just at daybreak, the plunder began, and
> was finished in short order. Everything was taken from them, and some
> of the boys were tied and held as slaves; the rest are in the bush, waiting
> to go to the king to hear the reason of the whole matter.[13]

The relative state of peace existing during Ekuikui's reign ended
in 1896 when his successor, Numa II, attacked the European fort.

The immediate cause of Numa's action was the arrival of a contingent of soldiers from Bié, on the way to the penal colony of Lobale. The king, not taking kindly to the presence of so many Europeans in his territory, gathered his warriors and on the night of March 7, 1896, entered the fort and set fire to the camp. Second Lieutenant Oliveira, in great alarm, rallied his soldiers, and ordered them to open fire against the rebellious king and his people. The commander of the fort hurriedly sent off messages to Bié and Benguela requesting military aid. From Bié came sixteen soldiers and a sergeant with 9,000 rounds of ammunition for their firearms. The beginning of May saw the destruction of the *ombala* (king's stronghold) of Numa.[14]

The last acts of rebellion of any consequence in Bailundu took place in 1902. African resentment against the unscrupulous practice of contract labor was the immediate cause. The rebellion spread beyond the Bailundu area and the Portuguese were forced to undertake military action. Three columns of soldiers were ordered to proceed to Bailundu: one from Lubola, under the command of Lieutenant País Brandão; another from Benguela, marching through Caconda under Governor Martinho's command; and another from Benguela, passing through Lobito with Massano de Amorin as commander. Portuguese arms effectively subjugated the rebellious *soba* (chief), Indungulo. Some fled south to the Bimbe region and continued to harass the Portuguese troops and settlers. Reinforcements arriving from Luanda in the beginning of 1904 subdued the rebels. A military post was established in Bimbe the following month. Bailundu was then considered occupied.[15]

The second military campaign of special note, the Cuanhama massacre of 1904, had its roots in the beginnings of the conquest of this southern section of Angola. It is difficult to fix the date when Portugal began to contemplate occupying this area. The earliest record is a letter written in 1850 by Abreu e Castro to the Conde de Castelões. Abreu e Castro had accompanied the governor of the district on a journey into the interior. He wrote to the *conde* stating that when the opportunity arises, Portugal should open relations with the more powerful of the *sobas* in the Cuanhama district.[16] Also in 1850, Bernardino Brochado mentions that the population in the Cuanhama could be calculated to be from 120,000 to 130,000 persons. He describes the *soba* thus:

> The present *soba* of Cuanhama is a man of about 75 to 80 years; of good health considering his age; always carrying himself with dignity, at times with great severity; uses few words, but with great expression and a certain arrogance; some of the people approach him in fear and trembling whenever they wish to speak to him. This is understandable since his powers are absolute. He can simply say, "Kill" and his command is carried out. He is proud and his kingdom is probably the largest in this area. Many fear him and acquiesce to his wishes whatever they may be.[17]

Portuguese penetration into this vast semidesert area was slow during these earlier years. Permission had to be secured first from the powerful Cuanhama *soba*, before any extensive journeys could be made. In 1852, Ladislau Magyar secured the help of Aimbiri, the Cuanhama *soba*, and made various exploratory trips into that region.[18]

Portuguese historians described the people of Cuanhama as warlike barbarians who liked to pillage and exterminate the villages of the surrounding areas. The Cuanhamas were responsible for the many attacks against Portuguese troops after the capture of Evale in the Cuamato region. An African rebellion was recorded in 1885, when a Catholic mission was destroyed and two French priests, Padres Luis Delpuech and Rothan, were killed. The constant harassments by the people of the Cuanhama region made it mandatory for government officials to take some strong military action.

The campaign of February 17, 1902, was one of the major campaigns in the subjugation of the Cuanhamas. The *chefe de posto*, or administrative head, of the district of Humbe, Lieutenant Artur de Morais, describes the battle in his book of memoirs as one of the greatest Portuguese victories, of great prestige for the Portuguese army. The engagement took place in the early hours of the morning of the seventeenth. Portuguese officers with the help of the Mundongas, traditional enemies of the Cuanhamas, encountered a great number of the enemies advancing cautiously through the tall grass. Without losing any time, the Portuguese forces opened fire. Caught by surprise, the Cuanhamas broke ranks and fled in

various directions. Later in the morning, at 10:15 A.M., the Cuanhamas regrouped their forces along the river. In the meantime the
Portuguese forces were reinforced by the arrival of the *chefe* of the
district accompanied by other Europeans. They brought a cannon
with them, and a steady volley of artillery fire and grapeshot com-
menced. An hour and a quarter later, the Cuanhamas were routed.
By 2:20 in the afternoon, the Cuanhamas' retreat was complete.
Fifty-eight men from the Cuanhama region were killed. Two of
the Mundongas were casualties on the side of the Portuguese. When
they returned to their home base, the Portuguese showed their gratitude to the Mundongas by giving them portions of *aguardente* (hard
liquor) because they had no other gifts. The Portuguese say that
this was not to be condemned, because for the Mundongas, no other
gift was more welcome than the *aguardente* offered.[19]

The "warlike and barbarous soul," nevertheless was uncon-
quered. In 1904 came the disastrous expedition under the command
of João Maria de Aguiar. The following description of the battle
of Pembe is recorded in the memoirs of Artur de Morais:

> The detachment of troops began its march at 6:00 in the morning.
> In the front marched an advanced guard of a platoon of cavalry and a
> native guide from Luanda who had been in Humbe and was said to be
> familiar with the Cuamato region. We first marched in a southeasterly
> direction and later directly towards the east. After marching for about
> two kilometers through dense woods which at times made it impossible
> to be in contact with the advanced cavalry, I requested permission from
> the commandant to go on ahead until I came into contact with our ad-
> vanced forces. This was granted and 2nd Lieutenant Faria Roby accom-
> panied me. We came upon a large green space and just ahead of us
> we saw two natives. Lieutenant Roby and I decided to take them as
> prisoners. As soon as they saw us, the natives fled. We raced our horses
> and as we neared them I yelled in their native language, which I had
> learned, "Don't flee. We do not intend to harm you. We only want
> to talk with you." But the natives continued to run. I spurred on my
> horse and cut them off from their course. As I did this, one of them,
> who was truly a giant, struck me on the chest with his *zagaia*. In re-
> taliation I slashed him with my sword. Lieutenant Roby helped me in
> overcoming him. A shot from my pistol ended the battle. The other
> native, in the meantime, had escaped.
>
> The shot from my revolver was the signal for the grand battle which

was to take place. In a few minutes the enemy surrounded us and opened fire. Our detachment arrived soon after. The enemy advanced slowly, keeping a steady fire upon us. It was now the responsibility of our cavalry to relieve us of the enemy's fire. The commander, Lieutenant Adolfo Ferreira, was hit first; then Lieutenant Reaende, followed by an enormous number of sergeants, corporals, and privates. The enemy's fire became more intense and our men began to feel afraid. Soon after, the order to retreat was given. Unfortunately this was done too late. We continued our fire, but our supply of bullets was low. When our troops realized that we were without ammunition, there was a moment of panic. The platoon of Europeans covered the retreat of our men, but this was of no avail. The enemy saw that we could not resist their attack too long, and fearing the arrival of reinforcements, charged upon us enmasse. We fought hand in hand with bayonets, pistols, hatchets, swords. Then "Oh, Crime! Oh Horror!" the enemy threw grenades in the midst of our European platoon, killing the commander of the artillery and Nunes of the dragon squadron and 22 guards.[20]

The battle of Pembe cost the Portuguese 300 men. Of these, 120 were Europeans. To avenge this defeat, Captain Alves Roçades in 1906 obtained permission to form an expedition consisting of 87 officers, 1,306 European soldiers, 906 native soldiers, 115 native auxiliaries, 57 civilians and 24 expatriates. Arms included 10 cannon, 54 machine guns, 1,602 rifles, 357 *solipedes* and 50 cars. The contingent was formed in Fort Roçadas. On August 26 they marched towards the principal *ombala* of the enemy. The following day, in the battle of Mofilo, the Portuguese defeated the 20,000 African defenders. The Portuguese considered this defeat as the end of the invincibility of the "warlike and ferocious" Cuanhamas.

The last military campaign of note, the Dembos occupation of 1907, was slow and tedious. Captain João d'Almeida, commander of the police, described the Dembos people as follows:

All the region between Zenza and Dande (almost at the portals of Luanda), from Sassa and the Morime lake to the southwest, are insubmissive, not even permitting Europeans to cross any of the rivers and to penetrate into their lands. Even the proper indigenous people are forbidden to bring any articles of trade to the Europeans. Adjacent regions of agricultural fazendas have turned into havens of refuge for contract fugitives, deserters, criminals, and even in Quillengues, we have received report that the condemned and deported have established themselves.[21]

The rebellious people, not content with controlling their own territories, began to plunder in the neighboring *sanzalas* (villages), and carried off prisoners for ransom. The historian Henrique de Paiva Couçeiro describes the Dembos people as naturally "rebellious and of untamed disposition." [22]

Between September 20 and December 8, 1907, a column of troops numbering about 550 men under the command of Captain John d'Almeida subjugated and occupied the Dembos. Captain d'Almeida described the physical obstacles of their campaign; mountains, valleys, rain and heat, all contributed to the hardships. Not counting loss due to illness or accidents on the march, the casualty list in combat was eighteen dead and forty-five wounded.

In 1908, on the order of the Dembo Cazuangongo, there began further harassment of Europeans in that area, principally technicians who were working on the railroad line. The government sent reinforcements under the command of Lieutenant Pina Guimarães, and the two forces engaged in combat. The rebels defended themselves fiercely, killing 20 per cent of the troops in a short time. Soon afterward, Cazuangongo fled to the mountains with his soldiers to wage guerrilla warfare. Three years of constant vigilance and policing were necessary to open the Dembos region for colonization.

The memory of these battles evokes different sentiments. Europeans look on them as heroic battles fought for the mother country. These feelings were expressed in 1932 when the minister of colonies, Professor Armindo Monteiro, visited the site of the 1904 Cuanhama massacre and held a commemorative service for the victims. The newspaper *O Seculo*, in its October 4 issue, reported the event:

A roll call of the dead was made, one by one. As each name was called, a marine guard answered, "Presente." When the last name was read, the company of soldiers presented arms, and sounded the clarions. The sun went down. No one talked. Soon after, among the great mass of Africans present, four elderly men advanced. They had taken part in the massacre of 1904. When they arrived at the base of the monument, they kneeled as a sign of respect and submission. No one had

provoked them to take this action. This was the best way to erase the
sad memory of those who had heroically died for the glory and splendor
of Portugal.[23]

Africans, on the other hand, look upon these battles as expres-
sions of their courageous resistance against superior armed forces.
Conquest was not due to the superiority of the Portuguese over the
Africans, but to the deciding factor of modern arms. African bravery
assumed its greatest height in these battles. The memory of the
"fallen warriors" remains alive among the African peoples. Africans
recalled the resistance of the Bimbe soldiers in the Bailundu campaigns of 1902 when, in 1957, a rumor spread through Bailundu
area that guns were found by the police in one of the Bimbe villages.
Africans whispered to one another, "The Bimbe people will rise
again. They were the last ones to capitulate."

## Present Tribal Status

By 1917 the Portuguese government could claim with certainty
the subservience of most of the tribes. The official census today di-
vides the ethnic groups into six divisions: Kikongo, Kimbundu,
Lunda-Chokwe, Mbundu (Ovimbundu), Nganguela, Others
(Cuanhama, Seles). The 1950 population according to ethnic groups
is shown in Table II.

### II. POPULATIONS OF ETHNIC GROUPS IN ANGOLA, 1950[24]

| Groups | Male | Female | Total |
| --- | --- | --- | --- |
| Kikongo | 220,759 | 259,059 | 479,818 |
| Kimbundu | 527,928 | 555,393 | 1,083,321 |
| Lunda-Chokwe | 173,989 | 183,704 | 357,693 |
| Mbundu | 721,213 | 722,529 | 1,443,742 |
| Nganguela | 159,088 | 169,189 | 328,277 |
| Lunyaneka | 54,345 | 54,455 | 108,800 |
| Lunkhumbi | 41,229 | 41,832 | 83,061 |
| Kuanyama | 28,923 | 33,218 | 62,141 |
| Herero | 12,198 | 12,986 | 25,184 |
| Others | 86,500 | 86,729 | 173,229 |
| Total | 2,026,172 | 2,119,094 | 4,145,266 |

The larger tribes are the Kimbundu, who live in a rectangular area in from Luanda and eastwards, and the Ovimbundu, who occupy the Benguela highland in central Angola. They comprise more than one-half the total population. No group can govern Angola without the support of these two groups.

Each tribal group has its modern economic, political and social character. The Kikongos, who number 500,000 and live in Portuguese Congo, are part of the Bakongo kingdom of the lower Congo. The wealth of the Kikongo people is derived from the cultivation of coffee. They live in better houses and some own automobiles. Politically, they are linked with the Bakongo party of the Republic of Congo.

South of the Bakongos are the Kimbundu-speaking people. They are more Europeanized. The capital city of Luanda and the inland town of Malange have influenced the life of these people. Generally, the Kimbundus speak fluent Portuguese and have many students in the *liceus* (high schools). They depend much more upon an economy based on the cities of Luanda and Malange. Politically, they are aware that independence is sweeping through Africa.

The Ovimbundu are less vocal in political matters than their northern neighbors, the Kimbundu. This is due largely to their geographical isolation from the coastal port of Luanda. Lobito, the terminus for the Benguela railroad, has provided some of the Ovimbundu educated elite opportunities of contact with other Africans. The economy is basically agricultural. Many contract laborers are recruited among the peoples of this group.

The Cuanhamas, who live in southern Angola, differ from the other tribal groups in that they are a cattle-raising people. Their life is seminomadic, and they are physically strong and handsome. Government officials often express admiration for their outward bearing and physical endurance. Because they live far from the major cities, the Cuanhamas are politically isolated from the currents of nationalism on the African continent. Independence to them means an independence which was in existence before the Portuguese occupied their land.

The Lundas are considered the most "primitive." They occupy the northeastern section of Angola and are isolated from the rest of the population. Few work in the cities. Many have employment at Diamang, the government-controlled diamond-mining company, which holds exclusive labor-recruiting privileges in the area. Officials of Diamang encourage the Lundas to retain their customs. For this purpose, the company established a museum at Dondo.

All five ethnic groups described here have a knowledge of each other's customs and habits. Intertribal wars have ceased. More and more we hear Africans refer to themselves as "*Nós Africanos*" (We Africans). Internal and external forces are bringing these tribal groups ever closer to each other. We shall now examine these forces.

# 2. PORTUGAL'S COLONIAL POLICY

## Justification

Portugal justifies her rights to govern her overseas territories on legal and moral grounds. Legally, Portugal points to the Berlin Conference which met on November 15, 1884, and to the agreement approved in final form on February 26, 1885. The declaration provides that "any power which henceforth takes possession of a tract of land on the coasts of the African continent, outside of its present possessions, and shall acquire it, as well as the power which assumes a protectorate there, shall accompany the respective act with a notification thereof, addressed to the other signatory powers of the present Act, in order to enable them, if need be, to make good any claims of their own." [1] Portugal's acceptance of the agreement of the Berlin Conference only confirmed her previous conviction of her right to govern these colonies.

Portugal refers to history and calls attention to the norms which were in existence from the fifteenth century to the nineteenth century. Dr. Marcello Caetano, apologist for the Salazar government, and once the colonial minister of that government, defines in his book, *Portugal e o Direito Colonial,* the international norms in fifteenth-century Europe, especially in the Iberian peninsula, where political and judicial ideas still possessed characteristics of the Middle Ages. International European society identified itself with a community of nations which was Christian, aiming for an organic, moral and political unity. The dream was to install the Pope as the supreme governor of this community. The task of the temporal nations, such as Portugal, was to implement and extend this community all over the world. The Pope, being the visible head of

Christianity, was the chief of the international society of potential Christians.[2]

This has been the spirit of Portugal's colonial policy. James Duffy in his book *Portuguese Africa* refers to it as the "heroic element." He quotes Jorge Ameal, writing in *O Mundo Português*:

> The evocation of our epic as sailors and warriors, the ancestral memory of an astonishing gallery of discoverers and builders, who, moved by a sacred impulse, carried to the ends of the world our ships, our dominion—and our faith. In this heroic element is contained the most noble sentiment of our mission as a chosen people, as an evangelizing people, since the task of civilizing must have, above all else, a spiritual content. The Portuguese, like no other people, made their enterprises of exploration and conquest a transcendent campaign, a sharing of spiritual values.[3]

The idea that Portugal's flag flies over three continents evokes a great feeling of pride in this small European power. Evidence of this sentiment was displayed in July 1954, when India questioned Goa's status. In Luanda, the chief coastal city in Angola, government offices, commercial and banking firms, shops and food markets were closed so that residents could participate in the protest rally directed at India held in front of the Governor's Palace. Speakers for the government exhorted the residents of Luanda to stand firm in this critical moment of Portuguese history. "Goa has been part of Portugal for four hundred years," the speakers said. "India has no right to claim her as part of her territory. We will fight and if necessary be willing to shed our blood for our Motherland."[4]

Portugal glories in the fact that her reign extends over such vast territories as Angola and Mozambique. This pride becomes understandable when one hears other Western nations refer to Portugal as a small, illiterate and backward country. The *World Book Encyclopedia* describes Portugal thus:

> Portugal is about the size of the state of Maine, but it has about nine times as many people. The Portuguese workers and farmers are very poor. They get little money and work long hours. It is all they can do to feed their families, which are usually large. The Government has done little to improve the lot of the common people. There is much disease, and social services are almost entirely lacking. Newspapers are

not permitted to print news which the government does not want the people to see. There have never been enough schools to educate all Portuguese children. Portuguese officials consider that anyone who can trace the letters of his name is a person who can write. According to this standard, about half the people of Portugal can read and write.[5]

To offset this relatively insignificant position in the council of nations, Portugal relives her history. The "heroic element" is necessary for Portugal to justify her claim to her overseas territories in Africa. Her overseas territories are essential to her national pride.

The "heroic element" also creates a paternalistic administrative government. It is similar to the relationship of a father to his child, of the learned to the ignorant, of the "advanced" to the "primitive," of the Christian to the pagan. Camoens, in his epic poem *The Lusiads*, expresses this sentiment in Canto X when he writes of Portugal: "This part is Christian Europe, more advanced and more renowned alike in its governance and its might than the others. Here is Africa, still grasping after the things of this world, uncivilized, full of savagery, with its southern-most Cape that has always been denied you until now. Look out over the whole vast continent and see how everywhere it is the home of legions of infidels." [6]

Out of these distinctions the Portuguese have evolved the "native policy" known as assimilation. The Portuguese never deny that Africans are members of the human race. But they do hold that the African is a child who needs the Portuguese to guide him to civilized European manhood. Therefore, for administrative purposes the government has two terms applicable to Africans. They are *assimilado* and *indígena*.

## The Assimilado

An *assimilado* has become "civilized" and "Europeanized." The primary requirement for the status of *assimilado* is the ability to speak the Portuguese language. Duffy cites the other requirements:

The applicant must be at least eighteen years of age. He must demonstrate that he earns sufficient income for himself and his family. He must be of good character and possess those qualities necessary for the exercise of the public and private rights of the Portuguese. He must not have evaded military service or have been declared a deserter. The candidate submits his application to the local administrative authorities who, after reviewing the case, decide whether to issue the proper identification card. The wife and children, legitimate or illegitimate, of the *assimilado* may acquire citizenship if they speak Portuguese and demonstrate their good character and the qualities necessary to exercise the right of Portuguese citizenship. These formalities may be waived and the *bilhete de identidade* issued to any African who proves that he has exercised a public charge, that he is employed in the colonial administrative corps, that he has a secondary school education, that he is a licensed merchant, a partner in a business firm, or the proprietor of an industrial establishment.[7]

To fulfill these conditions the applicant must possess a variety of documents. He must have a certificate of birth; certificate of residence, certificate of clearance from the Civil and Criminal Bureaus; certificate of good health; declaration of loyalty; declaration of literacy; and two testimonials of character. The acquiring of these documents require *paciencia*—patience. Often the date of expiration of a certificate prohibits the amassing of all the documents at one time. For example, the birth certificate is valid for three months. So is the health certificate. Because of bureaucratic inefficiency, a certificate may arrive after the expiration date of another document, thus necessitating starting the process all over again.

In addition to the virtue of patience, the applicant for *assimilado* status must have available cash. Official stationery, government stamps, fees to the notary public, all cost money. Some applicants hire an authorized agent, usually European, to process their application. Chances of success are greater if a European acts as the go-between. Handling fees range from 850 to 1,500 escudos ($30 to $50 in U.S. currency). The cost is high relative to the monthly cash income of most of the applicants. A schoolteacher in a mission school receives $17 (U.S.) a month. A telegraph operator on the railway may receive a slightly higher wage.

The advantages of an *assimilado* are many. He is free to travel in the country from one district to another without explicit permission from the administrator of his area. He is exempted from paying the *imposto,* or head tax. As he is supposed to be gainfully employed, he is exempted from contract labor. He receives equal pay with a European in a government job, if he has the necessary qualifications. During national elections he is given a ballot by which he can show his preference for the government's candidate.

In the presidential election of 1958 both government and anti-Salazar groups courted the *assimilados* for their votes. Often in the rural or town districts, the *assimilados*—without realizing it—held the deciding votes in determining whether a district was pro- or anti-Salazar. This was due to the limited number of registered voters in these areas. To win in a town with 150 European voters evenly divided between the two contestants, a candidate required the support of the fifteen or twenty *assimilado* residents of the district. The Bailundu district provided a good example. One hundred and twenty persons were registered as qualified voters. Of this number, approximately fifteen were Africans. The unpublished results gave government candidate Américo Tomás 65 votes. Humberto Delgado received 55 votes. The fifteen African votes as a "bloc" could have swung the election in either direction. But rural *assimilados* were not concerned with the outcome of the elections. Hence, many voted for the candidate of the European who offered to conduct him to the polls.

Many Africans voted in a presidential election for the first time in 1958. What was their reaction? Many *assimilados* were amused at their sudden importance in the national affairs of Portugal. They observed an anti-government party campaigning actively against the government. Two white groups were contesting with each other for power, and thereby destroying the Portuguese myth of "One Country, One Government, One Race." Voting awakened in many Africans the desire to participate actively in political affairs.

The *assimilado* has the same rights as a European, according to Portuguese civil law. Theory and practice are far apart, however, especially in personal relations. *Assimilados* continue to be addressed by government officials and European merchants by the second person *tu,* which denotes the teacher-pupil or master-servant relationship. "Right of Admission Reserved" signs in restaurants, theaters and clubs are safeguards against complete social integration. It is rare for an *assimilado* to challenge the right of the owner or manager of a theater to restrict admittance to these establishments. These restrictive signs persist in a culture which claims to be free from race consciousness.

It is true that there is less race consciousness in Portuguese Angola than in South Africa or in Southern Rhodesia. Blacks and whites mingle freely in public transports, in the market places, and in the commercial and banking houses. Furthermore, there is considerable intermarriage between the two races, a practice frowned upon by most other peoples. In many societies "miscegenation" is a fear-ridden word. White southerners in the United States say that they are against integration because they fear miscegenation. South Africa's policy of the separateness of races (*apartheid*) is justified on this basis. Products of miscegenation are called half-castes and half-breeds: words connoting scorn and degradation. In the Union of South Africa they are classed as "coloureds." Whatever the terms of classification, the products of miscegenation are the "outs" in both the white and black communities, in most societies. Both communities would like to forget them and erase them from the social organization.

The Portuguese, on the other hand, deny that miscegenation is an unhealthy practice. They humorously say that "God made white men and God made black men, but mulattoes were made by the Portuguese." Mulatto children (*mestiços*) are accepted in European society. If claimed by their European fathers, *mestiços* by law are Portuguese citizens. Many are employed in government services as postal clerks and civil administrative officials. The 25,000 *mestiços* in Angolan society are visible evidence of the mixing of the two races.

Dr. José Nunes de Oliveira, Inspector-General of Overseas Administration, in his address to the North American Assembly on African affairs, summarized the Portuguese feeling on race:

> The law, as a matter of fact, distinguishes citizens and natives, that is to say, civilized and non-civilized, refusing to the natives who remain attached to ancestral traditions, such as polygamy, the exercises of political rights characteristic of the institutions typically European.

But also in European Portugal the right to vote is refused to the illiterates who are not heads of family, on the understanding that they are not interested in using it or at least they could not make use of it conscientiously. The single fact of Europeans existing in similar political position to the Africans not civilized is enough to prove that the only distinction admitted by law is absolutely alien to racial considerations. It is not usual, I believe, to give firearms to children for playthings.[8]

In the official 1950 census 30,089 *assimilados* were recorded. The total African population of Portuguese Angola was 4,145,266. These figures indicate that slightly over one-half of 1 per cent of the African population are *assimilados*. The small number of *assimilados* raises grave doubts against the claims of the Portuguese that they are in Africa primarily to "Europeanize" the "natives" of Angola.

## The Indígena

At the other end of the scale is the *indígena* or the nonassimilated. His identification card is the *caderneta*. This category encompasses 99.3 per cent of the African population.

The underlying administrative policy of the Portuguese in the governing of the *indígenas* has been the adaptation of law to native customs. Decree No. 18:570, of July 8, 1930, Article 22, states: "Attention shall be paid in the colonies to the stage of evolution of the native populations, and there shall be special statutes for natives, which, under the authority of Portuguese public and private law, shall lay down juridical regulations for them in keeping with their individual, domestic and social usages and customs, provided that these are not incompatible with morality and dictates of humanity." [9]

What do the Portuguese mean by governing through their "individual, domestic and social usages and customs?" Administratively, the Portuguese use the tribal structure to govern the people. In doing so, however, the Portuguese have done away with the power and functions of kings. The influence of the hereditary Angolan kings, if any, is in the realm of memory and tradition. The *administrador* and the *chefe de posto* supplant him as the "king" of the area. The sub-chiefs and village headmen are pressed into service by the government for the assessing and collecting of the native tax (*imposto*), labor-recruiting both for government works and for private contracts. Often, in return for their services, the sub-chiefs and headmen (*sekulus*) are exempted by government officials from payment of the *imposto*. There is much injustice in the use of their responsibilities by these *sekulus*. It is usually the lowly commoner in the village who is called upon to do all the government chores. Bribery is widely practiced. As long as the *sekulus* do their jobs (that is, get men to do the necessary work), the Portuguese authorities usually ignore the injustices. They point to these as a natural attribute of the indigenous culture. Generally, the government *sekulus* are not loved and respected by the village peoples. On the contrary, they are much resented.

The *indígena's* position under the Portuguese common law, both civil and criminal, is precarious. The *indígena* is governed according to "regulations in keeping with their social customs and usages." [10] Administratively, the local government official, the *chefe de posto* metes out justice in civil cases. Often he is assisted by one or two Africans who may hold positions in the native police force or in the administration as clerks. These African helpers have acted as interpreters rather than intermediaries between the *indígena* and the government officials. The accused are not permitted lawyers for their defense. Interpretation of evidence and judgment rest upon one person: the local administrative official. Judgment is final unless the guilty person has fortitude to take a case from the jurisdiction of the *chefe de posto* to his immediate superior, the *administrador*. It is rare to have a decision made by a *chefe* reversed by the *administrador*.

Punishment is varied. Some may serve sentence by working for two weeks on a government project, either on a farm or on a building project. Others may receive the *palmatório,* beatings on the palms. Portuguese officials equate this practice to that of a parent disciplining his unruly child. Execution of these sentences, however, is in the hands of the "native" police, the *sepaios*. Portuguese officials and European settlers are officially discouraged from meting out physical punishment to Africans, to demonstrate "objective" treatment of the "native" population. *Indígenas* constantly face the threat of being sent off to some form of contract labor. Lately the Portuguese government has emphasized the voluntary aspect of contract labor (*voluntários*). However, the definition of voluntary is ambiguous, since the term does not mean the freedom to choose. All Africans are subject to contract labor unless gainfully employed. And "gainfully" is not defined to include the subsistence farming which is universally practiced by all the African villagers.

Many books and articles have been written about the evils of contract labor. In 1906, British journalist Henry W. Nevinson published *A Modern Slavery*, which documented the abuses committed in the name of contract labor in Angola and São Tomé. Seven years later, in 1913, John Harris wrote *Portuguese Slavery: Britain's Dilemma*. Harris stated that of the 70,000 to 100,000 Angola contract workers sent to São Tomé by the Portuguese during a period of thirty years, not a single worker had returned to his home in Angola. Another report was written in 1925 by Edward Alsworth Ross, an American sociologist. Dr. Ross, after a visit to Angola, published a report which described the deteriorating conditions associated with contract labor.

The 1947 report of Henrique Galvão, then Inspector of the Portuguese Overseas Ministry, drastically undermined the government's position in the practice of contract labor. Galvão concluded his report: "In some ways the situation is worse than simple slavery. Under slavery, after all, the Native is bought as an animal: his owner prefers him to remain as fit as a horse or an ox. Yet here the Native is not bought—he is hired from the State, although he is called a free man. And his employer cares little if he sickens or dies, once he is working, because when he sickens or dies, his employer will simply ask for another." [11]

In recent years, Basil Davidson, English writer and journalist, has continued in the tradition of Nevinson, Harris and Ross. In 1954, Mr. Davidson was commissioned by *Harper's Magazine* to visit Angola in commemoration of the fiftieth anniversary of Nevinson's report on the labor conditions in Angola. He too directed an angry tirade against the Portuguese government. Basil Davidson describes the theory of contract labor in these terms:

> Employers who want forced labour indent for it from the Governor-General. The Governor-General allocates *contratados* according to a theoretical calculation of the number available for conscription at any one time. Approved demands for forced labour—sometimes amended, sometimes (for bigger and wealthier private employers) imposing certain medical and housing amenities—are sent to local administrators up and down the country; and the *Chefe de Posto*, through his local chiefs and headmen, is then obliged to conscript the number of men required by the indent or indents which he receives.[12]

Africans generally agree that the recruiting system has become more humane in recent years. Native police are not sent out to comb the villages for manpower. Recruiting is done through government-certified European recruiters, who in turn use paid African assistants. Government regulations specify conditions of transport for these contract laborers such as the limitations in number, and the provision of benches in trucks. The *Código do Trabalho dos Indígenas* (the Native Labor Code), published in 1928, specifies the rules of conduct for African labor. The code is concerned with salaries; daily food rations which are furnished gratis by the employers; lodging and clothing; and free medical assistance. Abuses are corrected by periodic inspection by government officials from Luanda, the capital city. The year 1956 saw the wholesale transfer and eventual demotion of six administrative officials in the Bailundu *concelho* for illegal "trafficking" in contract laborers.

One thousand escudos ($35) is the usual amount received per head by the *angariadores* or European recruiters. A normal transport load is forty men. African recruiters receive 100 escudos, 10 per cent of the price paid per person, as their share. Letters to the editors in Angolan newspapers show that European men of the middle class—teachers, shopkeepers and clerks—resent the prosperity achieved by these European recruiters. Many abandon their jobs to join in what some Europeans call "mining black diamonds."

Recruiting of Africans for contract labor during the 1950s has been easier than in the past for two reasons. First, corn, the principal village cash crop, dropped to practically no market value, although it is now being exported again in quantity. Export trade statistics for 1938 and 1952 bear this out. In 1938, 129,745 tons of corn were exported; in 1952, 91,102 tons, a loss of 38,643 tons. Second, two severe drought years—1955 and 1957—were disastrous to village agriculture. A villager could earn cash income only by hiring himself out as a contract laborer.

The hardships brought about by contract labor are destroying African village life, especially in central Angola. Most of the able-bodied young men from the ages of sixteen to forty-five are engaged in this type of work. As a result, village after village is peopled with only the very young, the women and the old men. African family life suffers, as the men are away from their homes for periods of twelve to eighteen months.

The system of "voluntary" labor has contributed to the spread of nationalism, through the transportation of workers from the south to the coffee plantations in the north and to the docks in the two coastal cities of Luanda and Lobito. Workers have made contacts beyond their own tribal groups. Their realization of their common grievances over inadequate pay and bad working conditions has brought them the beginning of a feeling of solidarity against their European employers. These laborers are village peoples and will be found involved in any form of mass demonstration. The African party and trade union leaders can build upon the common feelings of antagonism of the *contratados* towards their *patroes,* or employers.

In 1948 and 1952, the Portuguese founded "native *colonatos.*" In contrast to the system of contract labor, the purpose of the *colonato* is said to be the preservation of the family and property, as well as the increase of production and the achievement of a higher level of living. The benefits from settling in these *colonatos* includes a house, storage barns, animal corrals and seeds. Cattle is also acquired for breeding and working. Ploughs can be borrowed for cultivating the soil.

There are two "native *colonatos*" functioning. The Caconda *colonato* was begun in 1948 with twenty families. This number increased to 730 in 1952, involving a total of 3,484 Africans. Over 5,500 acres are in cultivation and 111 miles of irrigated ditches have been opened. Construction included thirty warehouses, eleven houses for Europeans and eighteen "native" dwellings. One hundred more houses for "natives" will be built soon. Oxen, goats and pigs total 5,680. Maize, beans, rice, wheat and peanuts are the principal cultivated products. In 1952, 2,000 tons of maize were harvested.

The second *colonato* is located in Damba (district of Congo). The work was started in 1950, and 234 families were settled there by the end of 1954. The cultivated area totals 11,120 acres. Peanut, manioc and sweet potatoes are the principal products. There houses for Europeans, five warehouses for seed storage, and five tool sheds for storing agricultural equipment and machines have been built.[13]

The "native *colonatos*" are directed by an agronomist and a farm manager, both of whom are European. The maximum number of Africans involved in the two *colonatos* is 5,000. When compared with the total African population of 4,500,000, the government's program to develop African farms is indeed limited.

The Portuguese government's forced labor practices and the very small scale of its programs for the improvement of the conditions of Africans bring Portugal's colonial policy under severe criticism from Afro-Asians and from the Communist bloc. Furthermore, the rise of postwar nationalism heightened anticolonial feelings throughout the world. Africans questioned the right of European powers to remain in their countries. Thomas Hodgkin could write in 1956 of the following visible signs of postwar nationalism in Africa:

First, we have become accustomed to a succession of political explosions in Nigeria and the Gold Coast, in Uganda and Kenya; in the Sudan; in French West Africa (particularly the Ivory Coast); in the Union of South Africa. Second, during the past few years several new self-governing—if not fully sovereign—states have been brought into being. A third surface expression of the new nationalisms is the interdependence of happenings in the various African territories. Colonial frontiers no longer act as barriers to the spread of news and ideas.[14]

## The "New" Look

In anticipation of the growing criticism of her right to govern her African colonies, Portugal in 1951 changed their legal status from colonial possessions to that of overseas provinces. Articles 134 and 135, newly incorporated into the Portuguese Constitution, read as follows: "The overseas territories of Portugal are given the generic name 'provinces' and have a politico-administrative organization suitable to their geographic situation and their conditions of social environment . . . the overseas provinces as an integral part of the Portuguese state are linked to each other and to the metropole." [15]

Outwardly there were many manifestations of this new orientation. The heading on stationery of official documents changed from *Colónia de Angola* to *Província de Angola*. Many towns with indigenous titles, scattered throughout the countryside, were renamed. Names such as Bocoio, Catabola and Munenge have been replaced with these European names: Vila Sousa Lara, Nova Sintra and Vila Serpa Pinto. The hope of the administration is to link the old Portugal with the new through familiar Portuguese names. Often the government had to rescind the new name and revert to the old name because of the confusion created in the postal services. Such was the case with Andulo which changed its name to Vila Maçedo de Cavaleiros. It had to revert again to Andulo, because mail was being sent to Vila Maçedo de Cavaleiros in Portugal. On the whole the old *colonos* and Africans continue to refer to these places by their original names.

The "new" look also shows in education. In previous years the Chief Inspector of Schools of the Overseas Possessions had some latitude in the adaptation of the curricula to local needs, especially for Africans. The development of the *ensino rudimentar* with emphasis on the cultivation of the soil was an attempt to adapt education to local needs. In recent years, however, the trend has been to prescribe all school curricula in the offices of the Minister of National Education in Lisbon. One result is that all the exams in the schools from the third year up are formulated in Portugal. This is in line with the policy of keeping education uniform whether in Portugal or in her overseas territories. A routine matter such as the procuring of a teacher's certificate is now handled by the office of the Ministry of Education in Lisbon. This was formerly done in Luanda.

Another move to integrate the overseas provinces was the change from the Angolan currency of *angolares* to the Portuguese *escudos*. There was some resentment in Angola when the currency exchange ran 5 per cent in favor of the Portuguese escudos; that is, a 100 angolar note was worth about 95 escudos in Portugal.

Financially, the overseas provinces are closely tied to the mother country in spite of the fact that the *Carta Orgânica do Ultramar Português* recognizes the sovereignty of each province in the administering of its own finances. Such spheres as political missions of civilization, propaganda and study, and subsidies to companies of sea and aerial navigation continue to be the responsibility of the home country. Financial administration is also controlled by the Overseas Minister in Lisbon. Furthermore, all laws with respect to the budget of each province, including receipts and expenses, are similar to those of the home country.[16]

The criticism by residents in Angola that the trade balance favors the mother country is borne out by the following statistics. In the period from 1948 to 1952, imports from Portugal were 48 per cent of the total value of Angola's imports, Angola being the chief customer for Portugal's manufactured goods. In contrast, Angolan exports to Portugal represented only slightly over 25 per cent of Portugal's imports. Though the percentage of Angolan imports originating in Portugal has dropped since 1952, the home country continues to command a highly favored position in supplying Angola with her material goods, such as wine, textile goods and simple agricultural tools.[17] European residents of Angola say that Portugal needs them much more than they need her.

A further attempt by Portugal and a costly one—to integrate her overseas territory with the homeland—has been the policy encouraging the immigration of white Portuguese to Angola. The ten years from 1940 to 1950 show an 80 per cent increase in the white population in Angola. The 1940 census recorded 44,083 whites; in

1950 there were 78,826 whites. The flow of white immigrants during the years from 1950 to 1955 often reached one thousand each month.[18]

An important motivation for the flow of whites into Portuguese Africa is their poverty. The population in Portugal for the year 1958 was 8,980,000, a density of 25.4 persons per square mile. The per capita gross national product of Portugal in 1955 was $201. Belgium, a smaller European country with a population of 8,000,000 and a density of 763.1 per square mile, had a per capita gross national product of $1,015 for the same year. Portugal's $201 per capita gross national product reveals her poverty even more sharply when it is compared with that of a newly independent African country like Ghana, which in 1955 had a per capita gross national product of $135.[19] Problems involving employment, education and health services are enormous in an underdeveloped country such as Portugal. Portuguese Africa is the logical outlet for Portugal's problems of overpopulation and economic poverty. Furthermore, officials believe the increase in the number of whites is the quickest way to achieve the aim of integration, to make Portuguese Africa Portuguese.

There are two plans of colonization to settle the whites. The first is called *Colonato de Cela*. This project is located midway in a direct line from Luanda, the capital, to Nova Lisboa, in the interior. There is really no economic reason why the *colonato* was located there. Cela is far from the railroad or any other form of transportation by means of which *colonato* products can be sold reasonably. Luanda, the logical outlet for her produce, is over 300 miles away. During the November through April rainy season, the roads are almost impassable. There is a story that the governor-general thought of this scheme while flying from Luanda to Nova Lisboa, as he viewed this vast expanse of unoccupied land. It was from this that the idea of the Colonato de Cela was born.

With the Colonato de Cela, the white settler, for the first time in Africa, was not allowed to use native labor. The objective is to implant a Portuguese way of life, independent of African help. If the plan succeeds, Portugal can avoid the pitfall of South Africa's economic situation: the dependence of her economic well-being on native labor. The government has been very generous to these white settlers. Arriving in Cela, they are given about thirty acres, a house, some farm implements, seeds and two oxen. The government subsidy runs to about 175,000 escudos, or approximately $5,833. This sum has to be repaid to the government within twenty-five years. In the six-year period following the arrival of the first white settlers in 1953, the government had expended over $2,000,000 on this program in providing for a mere 300 families, numbering fewer than 2,000 persons.[20] Owing to the remote location, the settlers' lack of initiative, and their inexperience with farming on the African plateau, this project has been costly to the government. Moreover, the effect of this project on Africans has not been what the Portuguese authorities had hoped: a demonstration to the Africans of the superiority of Portuguese village life. It has been a revelation to the Africans to see barefoot, poorly clothed whites pasture their oxen on the grasslands, and to realize that the level of living of these whites is no higher than that of the advanced Africans. Many educated Africans speak and write Portuguese with greater facility than these *colonos*. The natives' belief in the superiority of the white Portuguese has crumbled.

The other colonization scheme is in the southern part of Angola and is known as the *Colonato de Baixa Cunene*. The railroad line running from the port of Moçamedes and through Sá da Bandeira and up to Vila Serpa Pinto gives the settlers a cheap means of transporting their produce to the cities or even of exporting it to Portugal. The hydroelectric dam of Matala furnishes electricity and irrigation for the *colonato* and for the city of Sá da Bandeira. There are approximately 200 families settled in this region and the administration hopes to reach the maximum number of 15,000 families as soon as possible. From the economic point of view, the possibility of success of this project is far greater than that of the Cela *colonato*.[21]

What effect has the "new" look on the Angolan Africans? Europeans say Africans are more prosperous and have more actual cash on hand. Many own motorized bicycles, phonographs and Western furniture. In line with the outward signs of economic prosperity, the Portuguese government increased the head tax from 150 to 225 escudos. Portuguese authorities justified this increase on the ground that the government's improved program of health and welfare for Africans required more money.

Politically, Africans remain in the same status. Fewer than 1 per cent have the right to vote. The other 99.3 per cent continue to exist as "children of the State." Professor Marcelo Caetano expresses the sentiment of the "New State" in these words:

Today the Portuguese universal ideal is still faithful to what it was in the 15th century, although, naturally, methods have changed. Portugal desires to be useful to humanity. She desires especially that the people who compose her political unity form part of a single spiritual family, believing that this communion of ideals and aspirations can but bring good to a world so tormented by the spirit of division. The ways of achieving and maintaining this moral unity may vary, and it is natural that the last word has not yet been spoken. But deep within each Portuguese there exists the firm determination to contribute towards maintaining forever the Portuguese community as a strong and living reality —a reality which, at the most critical moments of World History, may act as an important factor in the conservation or salvation of brotherhood and peace.[22]

Unfortunately, the words of brotherhood, peace and prosperity are interpreted to mean that Angola is a white man's colony. Africans point to the discrepancies in the wages paid to themselves and to whites. These discrepancies are real. Table III shows that European skilled workers earned three times the wage of Africans doing the same work in 1958.

### III. WAGES OF SKILLED WORKERS IN ANGOLA, 1958[23]

|  | European | | "Native" | |
|---|---|---|---|---|
|  | Escudos | Dollars | Escudos | Dollars |
| Compositors, manual | 4.500$00 | $157.50 | 1.560$00 | $ 54.60 |
| Compositors, mechanical | 5.000$00 | 175.00 | 1.200$00 | 42.00 |
| Carpenters | 3.120$00 | 109.20 | 1.690$00 | 59.15 |
| Cooks | 3.334$00 | 116.69 | 500$00 | 17.50 |
| Servants | 1.500$00 | 52.50 | 450$00 | 157.50 |
| Electricians | 3.080$00 | 107.80 | 1.030$00 | 36.05 |
| Plasterers | 3.640$00 | 127.40 | 1.560$00 | 54.60 |
| Office Workers | 2.500$00 | 87.50 | 1.800$00 | 63.00 |
| Stokers | 4.000$00 | 140.00 | 450$00 | 15.75 |
| Drivers of light vehicles | 2.500$00 | 87.50 | 1.200$00 | 42.00 |
| Stonecutters | 2.860$00 | 90.10 | 1.300$00 | 43.50 |

Furthermore, the state continues to limit education to a small number of Africans, as indicated in the enrollments in government and private schools according to race (Table IV).

| IV. SCHOOL ENROLLMENTS IN ANGOLA, BY RACE, 1958-1959[24] | | | | |
|---|---|---|---|---|
|  | Europeans | Mestiços | Africans | Others |
| Government | 11,043 | 3,323 | 801 | 3 |
| Private | 7,801 | 1,199 | 3,215 | 4 |
| Total | 18,844 | 4,522 | 4,016 | 7 |

In the year 1958-1959, African children beyond the *adaptação* level comprised one-seventh of the enrollment; Europeans, one-half. Four-fifths of the African enrollments were in private schools rather than government schools. Africans point to such figures as these to justify their belief that government policies are oriented towards the Europeans rather than the 4,500,000 Africans.

The Portuguese government's new social and political reforms for Angola assume that the overseas province is part of Portugal. On August 28, 1961, Overseas Minister Dr. Adriano Moreira declared in a speech to the Commercial Association of Porto (Portugal) that a new department of colonization would be created by the government. This department will seek to facilitate the integration of Angola into the mystique of the Portuguese multiracial society, and it will be immediately responsible for the study of ways in which soldiers in actual combat can be transformed into new settlers. In Dr. Moreira's words:

It is only in this way that the Portuguese can repeat the miracle which was realized in Brazil, where all barriers of race, color and creed disappeared. And it is within this spirit of fraternity that the government will abolish the status of *indígena* and extend citizenship to all Africans. Furthermore, new agrarian reforms will guarantee private property and the individual's right to farm his land.

Speaking of civil rights, Dr. Moreira announced that the proposed municipal laws will take into account those African traditions and customs which are not contrary to the moral principles of Christianity.[25]

Skepticism marked African reactions to the speech of the Overseas Minister. They cite the fact that the forced labor system was formally abolished by government decree in 1928, yet continues to exist under the name of voluntary labor. They also note that during the present crisis since April 1961, even assimilated Africans have been restricted in their movements. Local authorities require *assimilados* to apply for travel permits (*guias*) whenever they wish to leave their local areas to travel, for example, from Luanda to Nova Lisboa. Travel permits are required of *assimilados* even for such short distances as Bela Vista to Nova Lisboa (fifty miles). Before the crisis of 1961 only *indígenas* were required to carry travel permits. Under these circumstances, is it surprising that Africans doubt whether the social and political reforms proposed by Dr. Adriano Moreira will have any significant beneficial effect upon their lives? African doubts that the proposed Portuguese reforms will right what is wrong in Angola are increased by Dr. Moreira's statement that "our politics of today are the politics of yesterday." Africans say that the new reforms are *para os Ingleses ver* (for the English to see).

## 3. DISRUPTIVE FORCES

This chapter will examine the disruptive forces which modified the Angolan traditional society. First, the impact of Western education and the reasons Africans and the European power desire it will be explained. Then, the growth of towns and cities and their influence on African life will be discussed. Finally, the missionary movement—from which many Africans received new ideas and opportunities—will be examined.

### Education

Of the three interrelated forces—education, urbanization and the missionary influence—the thirst for Western education is the strongest. This is understandable, for education is the quickest route by which Africans can raise their status in the Portuguese society. Government positions in the postal, health and administrative services require the minimum of a fourth class diploma. Education is the key towards dignity, job opportunities, and economic wealth.

Not only Africans are interested in education. The Portuguese government also is concerned. Why? For one thing, they need governmental and postal clerks, telegraph operators, native police officers, for the administration of their colonies. Government authorities depend upon African interpreters who must be able to write and speak the Portuguese language. Again, to "Europeanize," to "Christianize" or to "assimilate" the natives, the Portuguese seek to impart to them a rudimentary knowledge of reading, speaking, writing and arithmetic. To achieve these two objectives, the Portuguese government has two distinct educational systems—one for Africans (*ensino de adaptação*) and the other for the white and assimilated Africans (*ensino oficial*). This distinction, they claim, is due solely to the "natural consequence of the degrees of social and mental development."[1]

The number of students enrolled in each section in 1956 is shown in Table V.

### V. STUDENT ENROLLMENTS IN ANGOLAN SCHOOLS, 1956[2]

|  | Schools | Teachers | Enrollment | Passed |
|---|---|---|---|---|
| Primário de adaptação | | | | |
| (missionário) | 1,042 | 2,560 | 49,142 | 36,180 |
| Elementary: | | | | |
| a. Government | 152 | 323 | 11,292 | 6,580 |
| b. Private | 177 | 367 | 8,324 | 5,604 |
| Technical | 12 | 148 | 2,164 | 1,310 |
| High School | | | | |
| a. Government | 3 | 65 | 1,730 | 1,000 |
| b. Private | 21 | 147 | 1,899 | 1,499 |
| Teacher Training | | | | |
| (missionário) | 1 | 9 | 183 | 143 |
| | | | | |
| Summary: | | | | |
| Government Schools | 169 | 525 | 15,270 | 8,826 |
| Missionary | 1,043 | 2,569 | 49,325 | 36,329 |
| Private | 203 | 551 | 10,618 | 7,335 |

According to the 1956 figures, 49,142 students were enrolled in the *ensino de adaptação*. Officially this section is the responsibility of the Roman Catholic missions. Article 24 of the Portuguese Colonial Act of July 8th, 1930, states: "Religious missions overseas, being instruments of civilization and national influence, and establishments for the training of personnel for service in them and in the Portuguese 'Padroado,' shall possess a juridical character and shall be protected and assisted by the State as institutions of learning."[3] Already in 1593 the idea of founding a *colégio* by Jesuit priests had been presented. Elementary education was started in 1605. A *colégio* was founded in 1607, and in 1619 four professors were installed: one in letters, two in Latin and one in morals.[4]

Protestant missionary societies also carry on an extensive educational program among the Africans. From their inception Protestant missions started schools. The American Board report of 1892 lists forty-two pupils in the boys' school. Their elementary course curriculum consisted of reading, writing and spelling. The years 1914 and 1916 saw the establishment of two training institutes for selected young men and women: Currie Institute for boys, with twenty-five pupils, and Means School for girls, with fourteen students.[5] The involvement of religious bodies in the education of Africans is revealed in Table VI.

### VI. ENROLLMENTS IN RELIGIOUS SCHOOLS IN ANGOLA, 1956[6]

|  | Sex | | Race | | |
|  | Male | Female | African | Mixed | Total |
|---|---|---|---|---|---|
| Catholic Missions | 26,833 | 12,016 | 38,411 | 438 | 38,849 |
| Protestant Missions | 7,547 | 2,746 | 10,261 | 32 | 10,293 |
| Total | 34,380 | 14,762 | 48,672 | 470 | 49,142 |

The increase in the number of schools and pupils in the *ensino rudimentar* (changed to *ensino de adaptação* in 1955) is indicated by comparing the 1952 school statistics with those of 1954. There were 500 schools in 1952; in 1954, 784 schools were functioning, an increase of slightly over 5 per cent. In 1952, 17,114 pupils attended classes; 24,618 pupils were recorded for 1954, an increase of over 40 per cent during a span of two school years. The rate of growth continues. But 49,142 African students in 1956 were few in relation to the size of the African population, for they comprised a mere 1 per cent of the total population in 1956.

The *ensino oficial* section for Europeans and *assimilados* is in a much more favorable position. From 1954 to 1956, government and private schools enlarged their educational facilities to accommodate the increased enrollment of students who came from European homes (Table VII).

### VII. ENROLLMENT INCREASE IN ANGOLAN SCHOOLS FOR EUROPEANS AND ASSIMILADOS, 1954-1956[7]

|  | Schools | | Teachers | | Students | |
|  | 1954 | 1956 | 1954 | 1956 | 1954 | 1956 |
|---|---|---|---|---|---|---|
| Primary | 139 | 152 | 293 | 323 | 10,979 | 11,292 |
| Technical | 5 | 12 | 61 | 148 | 950 | 2,164 |
| High Schools | 2 | 3 | 55 | 65 | 1,283 | 1,730 |
| Totals | 146 | 167 | 409 | 536 | 13,212 | 15,186 |

From the beginning the colonial government has obliged all schools to forego instruction through the vernacular and to employ the Portuguese language. Decree No. 77, specifically aimed at Protestant missions, clearly defines this regulation. Article 2 states: "It is not permitted to teach native languages in mission schools." Article 3 warns that "the use of the native language in written form or of any other language besides the Portuguese, by means of pamphlets, leaflets or whatever kind of manuscripts, is forbidden in the religious teaching (*catequese*) of the missions, in their schools, or in whatever relations with the natives." [8]

Such regulations make Portuguese the official and commercial language. Though civil administrative officials may use interpreters to deal with the village peoples, these officials utilize the Portuguese language as the principal medium of communication. To many Africans, learning to speak Portuguese has become a matter of prestige. Often European officials and settlers laugh at the efforts of the Africans to speak Portuguese and refer to their manner of speech as *pretoguese* (black Portuguese), a term equivalent to "pidgin" English.

As a result of the insistence of the government on the use of the Portuguese language, Africans have found a means whereby peoples from north, south and central Angola may communicate with each other. The possession of a common tongue has been a significant factor in the rise of nationalism in every African country dominated by a European power. The forty Africans sought by the Angola police in 1959 communicated with each other in Portuguese. Differences in linguistic structure between the languages of the five principal ethnic groups—the Kikongo, Kimbundu, Chokwe, Mbundu and Ngangelas—are distinctive enough to make it difficult for the Umbundu-speaking peoples to converse with the peoples from the Kikongo- or Kimbundu-speaking areas. A united Angolan nationalist movement would be impossible without a common tongue.

Education has also created a modern educated elite. This is a characteristic development throughout Africa. The elite group is small, but important in colonial Africa for several reasons: (1) the elite usually have sympathies and interests that go beyond the traditional tribal groups; (2) they possess the skills to run a modern nation; (3) they are interested in building nontribal organizations, such as political parties and cultural societies. These activities of the educated elites play an important part in modifying traditional village society. The village chief or headman requires help from someone who can read and write Portuguese. Administrative officials constantly demand statistics from the village *sekulus* (elders). Village Africans depend upon the educated elites for help in matters of birth certificates, paying of taxes and land registration. Petitions to government authorities must be drawn up by someone who can read and write. The status of the traditional headman is usurped in the villages by the young educated African. Often village Africans bypass the chief and request help from the educated elite in dealings with the government.

The creation of an educated elite has made Africans conscious of the inequalities of the Portuguese educational system. The division of schools into two sections—"native" and European education—is a source of irritation. They claim that the Portuguese are deliberately holding them back from entering into higher education. Africans point to Portuguese statements that rudimentary education is intended to "inculcate in the indigenous population working habits and aptitudes for driving them away from laziness, as well as for preparing the future rural workers and artisans." [9]

Africans also criticize the government for entrusting all education of natives to Christian missions. They maintain that the level of literacy can be raised only through schools sponsored by the government. Missionary societies have neither the resources nor the personnel to undertake such a broad program. They point to the many mission schools, especially on the village level, that lack basic school equipment.

Instruction for girls is another shortcoming in the Portuguese system. Of the 49,142 students enrolled in both Catholic and Protestant mission schools in 1956, 14,762—or 30 per cent—were girls. The percentage of *aproveitamento* or approval was also 30 per cent, indicating that African girls were as well adapted as African boys to master a European education. [10]

Concentration on primary education is also a handicap. The 1956 statistics show that 94 per cent of the school children were enrolled in primary education, either in the *ensino de adaptação* or

the *ensino elementar*. What accounts for this? First, education
after the fourth class is costly. The tuition of a private high school
is 5,000 escudos a year ($175). The added burden of boarding fees
puts the cost of a high school beyond the financial means of most
African parents. Second, the selective methods of the Portuguese
system limit the number who can receive high school education.
Every student, after the third year of elementary education, is required to pass the official exams before being admitted to the fourth
year. The average percentage of African students passing is 40
per cent in the third year (3a *classe elementar*) and 30 per cent in
the fourth (4a *classe elementar*).[11] The *liceu* (high school) examinations are far more rigorous, especially in the second- and third-year
cycles (fifth through the seventh years). In such a system Africans
suffer most. Language difficulties, unsympathetic teachers and
lack of housing facilities, are factors contributing to the small number of African students in the high school program.

Furthermore, the Portuguese government has discouraged the
creation of a university in Angola. The governor of the district of
Benguela, commenting upon the idea of a university in Angola,
remarked that there is really no need for such an institution because
Angola does not require a great number of African doctors, lawyers
or engineers. The demand, he said, is for laborers and artisans, and
hence the educational aspirations of Africans should stop at the
level of the trade or technical school. In spite of the many obstacles,
there are ten Angolan students studying in the professional faculties
in the universities of Lisbon and Coimbra. They are sponsored by
Protestant mission groups.

The inadequacies of the Portuguese educational system in
Angola are sensed acutely by the Africans when they compare it
with the educational systems of such neighboring countries as
Northern Rhodesia. In 1958 the total enrollment of all grades in
Northern Rhodesia was 248,905 students, or 11 per cent of the total
African population.[12] The same percentage in Angola, in 1956, was
1 per cent. Furthermore, the government of Northern Rhodesia
estimated that expenditure on education for 1959 was 2,767,729
pounds sterling (the equivalent of $7,749,641, or $4.02 per head of
the African population).[13] Angola's government grant in 1956 for
schools and professional institutions was 136,000 escudos (approxi-

mately $4,760.00, or one-tenth of 1 cent per head). The grant for
assistance to "natives" was much larger—7,711,000 escudos ($269,-
885 or 6 cents per head).[14] Such comparisons make Angola's Africans skeptical about Portuguese intentions to lift the level of literacy
in Angola.

## Vilas and Cidades

The second disruptive force is the growth of towns (vilas) and
cities (cidades) in Angola. Table VIII presents a comparison of the
population figures for various cities in the 1940 and 1950 census:

### VIII. POPULATION GROWTH OF ANGOLAN CITIES, 1940-1950[15]

|  | 1940 | 1950 | Percentage Increase |
|---|---|---|---|
| Luanda | 61,028 | 141,722 | 132% |
| Nova Lisboa | 16,298 | 28,297 | 73% |
| Malange | 5,299 | 9,473 | 80% |
| Lobito | 13,592 | 23,897 | 75% |
| Benguela | 14,243 | 14,960 | 5% |
| Silva Porto | 4,671 | 8,840 | 89% |
| Sá da Bandeira | 8,521 | 11,657 | 36% |
| Moçamedes | 4,926 | 8,567 | 73% |
|  | 128,568 | 247,152 | 92% |
| The racial compositions of leading cities (totals only): |  |  |  |
| Africans | 78,244 | 182,146 | 132% |
| Europeans | 22,289 | 45,450 | 103% |

Of the total population increase (11 per cent) between 1940
and 1950, 6 per cent—more than half of the increase—took place
in the cities. Of the 34,820 increase in the European population,
23,167 (or 66 per cent), occurred in the cities. Fifty-seven per cent
of the total European population in 1955 lived in cities, while only
6 per cent of the total African population were city-dwellers.

The increase in the population of cities is due primarily to the increase in economic activity, which is reflected in foreign trade statistics. The tonnage export for 1942-1947 was 2,048,168; for 1948-1952 it was 3,664,755, an increase of 78 per cent.[16] Agricultural products have dominated the items of export: in 1938 they represented 57.8 per cent of the total export value; in 1950, 79 per cent. The largest increase in agricultural export value was in coffee. In 1951 the total value in coffee exports was 1,527,724,000 escudos, or nearly 48 per cent of the total value exported for that year.[17]

The trend of the economy has made these cities into commercial, shipping and transport centers rather than industrial centers. Luanda provides a good illustration. The gross tonnage handled in the port of Luanda in 1948 was a little over 1,500,000; in 1952 it was more than 2,000,000—an increase of approximately 25 per cent during the four-year period. The increase in railroad tonnage handled was even higher—a 41 per cent increase.[18] Luanda is additionally the chief governmental, commercial and banking center. This accounts for the doubling of its population during the ten years ending in 1950.

The shift in the population from the rural to the urban areas is understandable. For the Portuguese in Angola there are two reasons, one economic and one social.

The struggle of the Portuguese to make a living in the *mato* (bush) has become increasingly difficult. The increased pressure for manpower under the contract labor system has reduced agricultural activities in the villages. Less land is cultivated and therefore there are fewer corn and beans to take to the European traders. The falling off in the production of these two cash products—corn and beans—has reduced the purchasing power of Africans. The low market value of the produce (except for coffee) has also reduced the trade volume in the village stores. The European trader's business stagnates. His only recourse is to extend credit, and this is precarious since payment depends upon a whole range of contributing factors: contract labor conditions, the world market, and stringent governmental controls on commerce.

Children of European farmers are not disposed to continue in their father's footsteps, even in projects like the Colonato de Cela. They feel that the meager income wrested from the land does not compensate for the amount of time and energy expended. An artisan in the city receives a minimum wage of sixty escudos for a nine-hour day. A farmer works twelve hours a day and may earn half as much if he is fortunate in producing a crop with a market value. Many ex-*colonos* are found in the cities of Luanda, Lobito and Nova Lisboa, as mechanics, chauffeurs, carpenters, plumbers and merchants.

Social factors also bring the Portuguese into the cities. The Portuguese are gregarious people, and isolation in the *povações* (small towns) increases the feeling of *saudades* (longing, homesickness) among them, especially among the womenfolk. The three or four Portuguese families in these small towns may or may not be congenial. Petty grievances assume enormous proportions in such a limited community. Traders and farmers in more remote sites often become more "Africanized" in their personal and social lives as the years go by. For many the only alternative is to return to the larger towns and cities. The homeland can be recreated far easier in Luanda, Lobito and Nova Lisboa.

Africans also have their reasons for moving to the cities. The unproductive soil has caused many to seek employment in urban areas. Many want money to pay for food, clothing, school fees and bicycles. Stories brought back by returning contract laborers from Lobito and Luanda of tremendous job opportunities ferment the desire of Africans to migrate to these cities. These laborers bring word that *continos* (porters or messengers) working in commercial firms earn wages of at least 400 escudos a month. An ordinary worker in the villages is fortunate to earn half that amount.

Another reason is schooling, especially on the *liceu* or high school level. Many who fail the third or fourth years in the elementary program go to the cities to take special exams. The regular school examinations are offered once a year. Students failing them have to wait until the following year. The department of instruction, however, has set up periods of *exames extraordinários* for those who are beyond the regular school age limit. Opportunities to attend night school also attract young Africans. After finishing their elementary education, many go to the cities where they work as messengers, clerks and porters during the day and attend evening classes in the various *liceus*. This is not possible upcountry.

A further motive is to escape the tribal authority in the villages.

Many flee from the *sekulus* after being nominated to do contract labor on government roads, farms and public work projects. Debts with local merchants also cause many to consider the cities as havens of refuge.

Whatever their motives in moving, Africans have been tremendously influenced by the change from rural to urban society. John and Rena Karefa-Smart of Sierra Leone say that

the city or large town, by its complexity and because it makes no provision for the extended family to maintain its physical integrity, forces the African to adopt an individually oriented way of life. Thus he depends less on the family and is not as strongly controlled either by the family or by the tribe. Added to this is the entirely new set of values based on working for a wage or salary and in activities that cannot clearly be seen to have any direct relationship to one's own life. Old religious ties are broken and in many instances, no new ones fill the gap.[19]

Beyond the effect of the weakening of family ties and traditional authority, the urban society has given the educated elite of the different tribal groups the opportunity to communicate with each other. In Luanda members of the Kikongo-, Kimbundu- and Umbundu-speaking peoples are grouped together in the Museque, the African section of the city. This is also true in Lobito. Cuanyamas, Ovimbundu and Chokwes emigrate there for various reasons. They reside in the African section called the *sanzala*. Tribal association groups exist in both of these cities. However, communication among these groups is in the colonial language—Portuguese—which has become the *lingua franca* of the country.

The location of both Luanda and Lobito as coastal ports has opened contacts between Angolans and educated Africans from other countries. In 1957 a group of Africans from Ghana participated in a workers' study conference at Luanda. This occasion gave some Angolan elites opportunities for conversation with the delegates from Ghana. The immediate result of this encounter was the apprehension of four Africans by the Policia Internacional de Defesa do Estado. The news of the arrests spread throughout the country, and the leaders of nationalist organizations considered that the arrested men had placed themselves in the vanguard of the fight for an independent Angola.

The concentration of educated Africans in urban localities intensifies their personal, social and economic grievances. *Assimilados* resent the paternal attitude of the Portuguese, their own "voluntary" segregation into "native" sections, and the limitations on their schooling in the Portuguese educational system. Furthermore, the influx of white Portuguese into the cities has made job competition between blacks and whites much more intense. Urbanization creates and magnifies all the problems arising from the uneasy relationship between Africans and Europeans. The result has been a closing of ranks among the Africans. Tribal and personal differences become insignificant. The modern educated Africans become anticolonial and anti-European.

## Planting of the Cross

The third disruptive force—the missionary movement—has been a part of Portuguese colonial policy since the beginning. It was behind Prince Henry the Navigator's order to "plant the cross on every headland," an order carried out by Portuguese sailors throughout the fifteenth century. In 1483, Diogo Cão, one of Henry's pupils, erected a *padrão*, a stone pillar emblazoned with the arms of the Portuguese monarch and surmounted by a cross, to signal occupation for Portugal and for Christianity.[20]

The obligation to convert the "heathens and infidels" was entrusted to the Roman Catholic church, the state church. The toll upon the Jesuit's first missionary efforts was high. Up to 1593 the Society of Jesuits had sent twenty-six priests to Angola. Of these only twelve were found still in service after several years. Eleven had died and the others returned to Portugal for reasons of health.[21] At the end of the eighteenth century there were Franciscans, Carmelites and Capuchins, besides the already established society of Jesuits in Angola. In the last half of the nineteenth century, in response to a plea from the Portuguese government, Rome sent French missionaries belonging to the Order of the Holy Ghost. They held the unique position of not being under the jurisdiction of the bishop of Angola, instead of which they were directly responsible to Rome.[22]

The Berlin Act of February 26, 1885, gave Protestant missionary societies their first opening to work legally in Angola. Article VI of the provisions, relating to the protection of the "natives," missionaries and travelers, and to religious liberty, states:

They [i.e., all signatories] shall, without distinction of creed or nation, protect and favor all religious, scientific, or charitable institutions, and undertakings . . . which aim at instructing the natives and bringing home to them the blessings of civilization. Christian missionaries . . . shall likewise be the objects of especial attention. Freedom of conscience and religious toleration are expressly guaranteed to the natives, no less than to subjects and to foreigners.[23]

Missionary efforts grew in number and success, until in 1950 approximately 50 per cent of the total population indicated in the census that they were Christians. Table IX shows the breakdown of Christian religious groups in this census.

IX. CHRISTIANS IN ANGOLA, CENSUS OF 1950[24]

| | Civilizados | Não-civilizados | Total |
|---|---|---|---|
| Catholics | 122,737 | 1,380,126 | 1,502,863 |
| Protestants | 8,691 | 532,621 | 541,312 |

Since the Roman Catholic church is an integral part of Portuguese government and culture, most Europeans are affiliated with the state church.

Both the Protestant and Catholic missionaries have been successful in converting large numbers of Africans to Christianity, but many observers have questioned whether African life has actually been penetrated by a Christian spirit in matters of faith and morals.[25] But there is no doubt that in many regions of Angola missionary activities have led to the modification of the Angolan African traditional society, through education, through the weakening of traditional authorities, through the introduction of the ideal of equality, and through the creation of an African clergy.

The church supplants the traditional kings and elders as the highest authority. Loyalty to the church comes to transcend kinship and tribal ties. Christian ideals, such as the worth of each individual in the sight of God and the love of one brother for another regardless of race or color, have appealed to the African's longing to be free from bondage to the white man and have constituted revolutionary influences in African life. But difficulties arose for the Western representatives of Christian churches when the Africans equated Christianity with European power. The contradiction between equality before God and discrimination among men, a contradiction inherent in the colonial situation, troubled both Catholic and Protestant mission societies.

The educational efforts of the various Christian missionaries have been at least equally effective in altering native life, since the Africans want education, even when they hold Christianity suspect. Article 24 of the Portuguese Colonial Act permits religious missions overseas to train African personnel for various offices in the Christian church. Early records show that the Roman Catholic church has from its first entrance into Angola sought to establish an African clergy. Young men selected by European superiors in the 1600s were educated in Portugal and afterward in Brazil. Candidates for the clergy were either African or mulattoes, many of whom were descendants of the old Jewish residents of São Tomé Island, who had been sent there by the Portuguese in the last decade of the fifteenth century. With the founding of a *colégio* by the Jesuits, the problem was partially resolved. Future clerics were sent to the *colégio*, but the Catholic church's ideal of a proper seminary in Africa for the training of African clergy was never realized.

At a later date Protestants also became concerned with the creation of an African clergy. Various mission societies founded Bible schools. Establishment in 1911 of the Dondi Schools, a boys' school and a girls' school, in central Angola was a step forward in the training of an educated Protestant community. These schools follow the official government curriculum: Portuguese, mathematics, science, history, morals and civics. The Ministry of Education allows Protestant schools to teach their own religious doctrines.

During the 1950s both Catholics and Protestants have accelerated their programs for the training of African clergy. Catholic seminaries in Luanda and Nova Lisboa are now the two principal

Catholic training centers. The Emmanuel Seminary in Dondi continues as the center of Protestant theological studies. Protestant African clergy presently number 130; African Catholic priests, over 300. The rise of an educated clergy has had a considerable impact upon the traditional society. Priests and ministers are not considered bound to the traditional authority of the kings and chiefs; indeed they often have become leaders of opposition. African clergy also have status as black men in a white society. African Catholic priests have sometimes possessed sufficient status to oppose the local administration, especially in cases involving members of their parishes.

Neither the Catholic nor the Protestant church in Angola has as yet taken a definite stand on the issue of nationalism. Officials of the Catholic church, by virtue of that church's ties with the state, tend to support the Portuguese government. Unquestionably, the Catholic church's ties with the state prejudice its future in Angola. As the struggle in Angola intensifies, Africans will look upon this association as Catholic sanction of Portuguese colonial policy. But no one knows how long the Catholic church will continue to support the Salazar government and its colonial policies. The dissociation of the Catholic church from the state would be of far-reaching significance in Angola. It would remove the moral sanction of continued Portuguese rule in Africa and would give moral support to those African Catholics in Angola who are working for independence.

The Protestants have no such official ties. Instead, Protestant missions have been accused by the Portuguese of "denationalizing the natives." [26] The Portuguese point out that Protestant missionaries introduce their own national cultures—British, American, Canadian or Swiss—and so wean Africans away from Portuguese national standards; and that they use the native languages in communicating with Africans, thus impeding the implantation of Portuguese language and culture. Article 2 of the Portuguese Colonial Act states that "it is not permitted to teach native languages in mission schools," but Article 3 states that the use of the native language is allowed "orally in religious instruction (*cataquese*) and as a help during the elementary period of teaching the Portuguese language." The great majority of Protestant religious services in the villages are conducted in African languages.

Are political forms possible through which Christian institutions may be used by Angolans to express their discontent? Thomas Hodgkin reminds us that

the tradition whereby Christian institutions and symbols serve as a form through which men express their aspirations for social and political change is as ancient as the Church itself. Since the Donatist revolt in fourth-century North Africa, a succession of Christian sects have combined separatism (in effect, if not in intention), on matters of Church organization with demands for social justice, stated in the language of religion. It is understandable that, in the conditions of twentieth-century Africa, the sense of oppression by colonial authority, and the moral crisis accompanying the disruption of tribal society and the invasion of commercial values, should have combined to produce movements of the same separatist type within the African churches.[27]

After studying the parallels between African mass party structures and the structures of the existing church organizations in Angola (both Protestant and Catholic), I believe that mass parties could evolve from church organizations in Angola. And we know that mass parties sparked the independence movements in Ghana, Guinea and Mali. This is also possible in Angola.

How do Angolan church organizations resemble in structure the African mass parties? Both Protestants and Catholics recruit members from all sections of the population, collect dues from them, educate them, and form from them a leadership elite. Let us observe the close parallels that exist between the institutional structure of a typical Angolan Christian church and the institutional structure of African mass parties, as those are described by Ruth Schachter in her paper, "A Note on the Classification of Political Parties in French Speaking West Africa." [28]

PARALLELS BETWEEN THE INSTITUTIONAL STRUCTURES OF
WEST AFRICAN PARTIES AND ANGOLAN CHRISTIAN CHURCHES

| Mass Party Structures | Angolan Church Structures |
|---|---|
| 1. The mass party seeks at the local level the adherence of every individual and seeks to establish local branches with local headquarters. | 1. The basic aim of the church is to bring the "gospel" to every individual, rural and urban, and the church forms local centers appropriate to this aim. |

*Mass Party Structures*

2. Leadership in a mass party is not vested solely in one person and does not depend solely upon kinship ties. A personal defection from the party rarely leads to the disintegration of even a local organization.

3. Mass parties encourage regular meetings and elections for branch leaders.

4. Mass parties call forth considerable direct participation from their members.

5. Mass parties usually create parallel women's and youths' organizations.

6. Officers of mass parties must give account of their stewardship.

7. Discipline is given serious attention in mass parties.

8. Mass parties publish newspapers, establish regional and central headquarters, hire party staffs, distribute membership cards and charge dues.

*Angolan Church Structures*

2. Leadership in the local village church, because of its rigid moral code, passes through many people. Leaders create positions for assistants. The local leader, the catechist, may appoint a catechist's assistant. Assistants are similarly appointed by choir leaders, by boys' leaders, and by girls' leaders.

3. Regular worship services are held every Sunday morning, and these are usually preceded by sessions of the church school.

4. All church members are urged to participate in the deliberations concerning any church business.

5. Churches hold women's meetings weekly in the larger villages. All pastoral areas have women's leaders who rally women for various projects. There are large Christian youth groups composed of the less educated boys and girls, although the chief strength of youth groups is in the upper elementary and *liceu* groups.

6. Church leaders must give a financial report at least annually.

7. Discipline is one preoccupation of church leaders, especially during their meetings. Members and leaders found to have broken church rules are disciplined.

8. Churches form area councils encompassing twenty to thirty villages, and form district councils encompassing seven to fourteen areas. Eight district coun-

*Mass Party Structures*                *Angolan Church Structures*

cils make up the general council.
Catechists are hired at the village
level; deacons and pastors at the
area level; a general secretary at
the regional level. Members receive a membership card when
they are received into the church,
and must renew the card each
year. Monetary contributions are
solicited from each member.

9. Mass parties are interested,       9. The Christian community at-
not only in electoral success, but    tempts to treat all aspects of life,
in all affairs of their members       from birth to death, within the
from the cradle to the grave:         church structure. Church coun-
birth, initiation, religion, mar-     cils concern themselves with
riage, divorce, dancing, song         schools, health clinics, hospitals,
plays, feuds, debts, land use and     feuds between members and some
ownership, migration, public or-      limited welfare projects.
der and death.

But mass parties also differ from the Angolan churches. Mass
parties, particularly prior to achieving government majorities, employ
techniques related to their revolutionary functions. Demonstrations,
strikes, boycotts and occasional violence are used as techniques of
revolution. In the church council, revolutionary concepts are not
prevalent. Mass demonstrations and boycotts do not underlie the
basic structure or strategy of the church organizations. The ideal of
rational discussion is dominant in the life of the church. The goals of
mass parties and church organizations are also different. The objective of the mass party is the formation of a political unit. The aim of
the church is to "plant the Church of Jesus Christ."

Mass parties and Christian churches can exist side by side;
members can participate in the activities of both. But one cannot
assume the functions of the other; the mass party cannot become the
church and the church cannot become a mass party, although its
members may join mass parties. Religious organization may have
political consequences in Angola, as economic organization has had

political consequences in other African nations. The *Rassemblement Démocratique Africain* had its foundation in the African planter's organization. Trade unionists were prominent within the *Parti Démocratique de Guinée.*

The Portuguese government is aware of the potential threat to colonial rule from existing Protestant and Catholic organizations. In a recent directive the governor-general ordered local administrative officials to attend all church meetings held in their juridical areas. This order was carried out at the last church council meeting of central Angola (Protestant), held in Dondi, Bela Vista, in January of 1961. The Administrator and the Inspector of Service of National Instruction, Dr. Rosa, sat in all of the sessions. Africans took advantage of the presence of the two government officials to petition the governor-general for a school aid grant to raise teachers' salaries in Protestant mission schools.

## 4. ANGOLAN NATIONALIST GROUPS

There are two nationalist groups in Angola, European and African. Europeans generally think of independence as the route to becoming another Brazil. They visualize Angola as the third party in the Luso-Brazilian community. Africans, on the other hand, see independence as part of the struggle for an independent Africa. The idea of a Lusitanian community does not excite them.

Yet both groups have in common their desire to be free from the Salazar regime in Portugal. So far this has been the basis for cooperation between the two groups. A coordinating committee, functioning in England, publishes the *Portuguese and Colonial Bulletin*, a monthly publication containing news of events in Portugal and the Portuguese colonies. "It is aimed to give a comprehensive and reliable service of information for journalists, diplomatists, libraries, university teachers, research organizations, state and political organizations and individuals interested in the economic and political situation in Portugal and her colonies, and in the development of movements against the dictatorship of Dr. Salazar and for the national independence of the colonies." [1] Contributors include both Africans and Europeans.

The nationalist groups, however, are distinct in character and organization. Each movement must be examined separately. We shall look first at European nationalism.

### European Nationalism

Three factors in a colony are conducive to separatism from the mother country: the geographical distance, the economic development and the creation of an "indigenous" European society. All three elements exist in Angola.

Geographically, Angola is 4,000 miles from Portugal. Ships and airplanes link the two countries, but the distance separating them impedes the development of a homogenous community. No matter how much the Portuguese may insist to the contrary, the overseas province of Angola is not in the same category as the domestic provinces of Minho or Algarve. The 4,000 miles contribute to the feeling of separateness.

Economically, Angola is not dependent upon Portugal. On the contrary, Angola is an important outlet for Portuguese goods. From 1943 through 1947 the percentage of the total import value from Portugal was 60.1 per cent. In the same period Portugal received 37 per cent of the value of the total exports. Succeeding years indicate that the mother country has become less important to the economy of Angola. The figures in Table X show other countries replacing Portugal as the principal partner in trade relations.

### X. CHANGES IN ANGOLAN FOREIGN TRADE, 1943-1947 AND 1948-1952[2]

|  | 1943-1947 | | 1948-1952 | |
|---|---|---|---|---|
|  | Imports | Exports | Imports | Exports |
| Portugal | 60.1 | 37.0 | 48.0 | 25.6 |
| Foreign Countries | 38.9 | 56.0 | 51.2 | 69.9 |

Angolan commercial firms prefer trade with foreign countries. The home country market is limited. Even Europeans in Angola see no advantage in being tied to the economy of Portugal.

Second- and third-generation Angolan Europeans belong to Angola more than to Portugal. Discrimination by the Portuguese against Angolan Europeans over a period of many years has made the ties to the mother country weaker for the Angolan Europeans than for the new *colonos* or settlers from Portugal. Angolan Europeans resent the fact that metropolitans consider them second-class Portuguese. Prior to 1950 the *bilhete de identidade* of Angolan Portuguese was not valid in the homeland. Restrictions on travel to Portugal applied to them as it did to non-Portuguese residents in Angola.

The demand by Europeans for autonomy began in the field of administration. The Pro-Angola party was formed in the colony in the early 1920s. The organization's manifesto proclaimed that the colonial administration had not satisfied the aspirations of Angolans, but recognized that Angolans are not in a position to realize their ideal: the establishment of administrative and financial autonomy based upon the British system of self-government. This autonomy, the manifesto stated, should be instituted as soon as economic, intellectual and moral conditions permit. The authors conceded that Portugal would continue to have sovereignty over Angola, but they wanted the colony to have the right to choose its own governor.

The government's reaction to European separatism was to state that Angola did not need greater autonomy but more competent technicians, capable of transforming the economy of Angola within the precepts of an honest administration. There was already autonomy in each of the five provinces, which were held together by a high commissioner representing the metropolitan government.[3]

The coming to power of Salazar in 1933 forced many democrats in Portugal to leave for Brazil and for Portugal's colonies. After World War II, Angolan residents formed underground opposition groups as overseas units of the metropolitan political parties. The presidential elections of 1958 gave the Portuguese opposition the first actual opportunity in seven years openly to oppose the government in power. Active antigovernment groups supporting the candidacy of General Humberto Delgado were formed in Luanda, Lobito, Benguela and Nova Lisboa. Local committees supporting Delgado were set up in every district. For the first time, village residents took an active part in opposing the government's candidate, Rear Admiral Américo Tomás. Leaflets were distributed throughout the countryside. Rallies were called by supporters of both parties. The rallies called for the support of Humberto Delgado were surprisingly well attended. Large advertisements in newspapers publicized the candidacy of Humberto Delgado. To counteract the fervor of the Delgado group, the administration utilized existing Juntas or associations sponsored by local governments to support their candidate. Members and their families were urged to work for Admiral Tomás and the União Nacional party.

Official results of the election were not published. Humberto

Delgado was reported to have 236,528 votes against 758,998 votes for Admiral Tomás, or approximately 23 per cent of the total electoral votes. Europeans in Angola said that Delgado received a majority of the votes cast in Angola. After the elections, there were several noticeable transfers of government doctors, nurses and postal clerks to remote administrative districts. Their crime was voting for Delgado. Other active Delgado workers curtailed their political activities, though many continued to hold an anti-Salazar point of view. In March 1959 seven Europeans were arrested and accused by the government of working against the "external security of the State of Portugal." Dr. Julieta Gandara, a well-known pediatrician in Luanda, was one of the seven. Another incident was the seizure of the liner *Santa Maria* by Captain Henrique Galvão in January 1961. This dramatic episode became front-page news.

Who is Henrique Galvão? And what has he accomplished? Henrique Galvão participated in the coup d'etat of 1926. He is a professional soldier and has held several offices including that of director of the Portuguese national radio. Captain Galvão ran afoul of the Salazar regime when in 1947, as chief inspector of colonial administration, he wrote a report condemning the forced labor practices in Angola. In 1951 he supported Admiral Quintão Meireles as the opposition presidential candidate. At the last moment Admiral Meireles withdrew his candidacy because there were no guarantees that a free election would be held. When Henrique Galvão attempted to form an opposition group, called the Portuguese Civic Organization, to unseat the Salazar government, the Policia Internacional de Defesa do Estado raided the office. Galvão was arrested and on December 9, 1952, was sentenced to three years' imprisonment. At a subsequent trial in 1955, he was accused of further subversive activities and sentenced to sixteen years in prison. Four years later he made his escape by putting a dummy in his bed and applied for political asylum at the Argentine Embassy in Lisbon. In May 1959, he flew to Argentina. Several months later Galvão went to Venezuela. It was there that he and his friends plotted the seizure of the *Santa Maria*.[4]

What were the purposes of this Latin drama? First, it was to call the attention of the world to the dictatorial regime in Portugal; second, to rally into one cohesive group the anti-Salazar groups scattered around the world. The first objective was realized without too much difficulty. The world press, radio and all other means of communication were utilized to cover this bizarre episode. Salazar and his dictatorial government were front-page news during the two-week period.

The achievement of the second objective, to rally the anti-Salazar groups scattered around the world, is more difficult to measure. A prominent citizen of Lisbon said, "This business is far from being ended. That is one thing you can be sure of." Captain Galvão will be remembered as a David waging battle with a Goliath.

The arrest by PIDE of the seven Europeans in March 1959 and the attempt of Captain Henrique Galvão to overthrow the Salazar regime in January 1961 are signs of deepening rift within the Portuguese community. European nationalism may bring the goal of an independent Angola much nearer. In the last analysis, however, independence for Angola rests with the Africans. They comprise 96 per cent of the total population and no government can govern Angola without their consent.

## African Nationalism

The earliest recorded modern African organization is the government-sponsored *Liga Africana*. At the Third Pan-African Conference in Lisbon in 1923, attended by representatives of eleven nations, Deputy Magalhães of the Portuguese National Assembly made this statement on the aims of the Liga:

The great association of Portuguese Negroes, with headquarters at Lisbon, called the *Liga Africana*, is an actual federation of all the indigenous associations scattered throughout the five provinces of Portuguese Africa and represents several individuals. The *Liga Africana* has a commission for all the other native organizations and knows how to express to the government in no ambiguous terms, but in a dignified manner, all that should be said to avoid injustice or to bring about the repeal of harsh laws. That is why the *Liga Africana* of Lisbon is the director of the Portuguese African movement, but only in the good sense of the word, without making any appeal to violence and without leaving constitutional limits.[5]

Two former colonial ministers also spoke at this gathering. Ironically, the recommendations of the conference seemed out of tune with the statements of the Portuguese officials. Africans demanded: (1) a voice in their own government; (2) the right of access to the land and its resources; (3) trial by juries of their peers under established forms of law; (4) free elementary education for all, broad training in modern industrial techniques and higher training of selected talent; (5) the development of Africa for the benefit of Africans, and not merely for the profit of Europeans; (6) the abolition of the slave trade and of the liquor traffic; (7) world disarmament and the abolition of war, but failing this, and as long as white folk bear arms against black folk, the right of blacks to bear arms in their own defense; and (8) the organization of commerce and industry so as to make the main objects of capital and labor the welfare of the many rather than the enriching of the few.[6]

The recommendations of the Third Pan-African Conference were ignored by the government-backed Liga Africana. In Angola the functions of the Liga are concentrated in the health, welfare, cultural and social spheres. Evening classes with emphasis on such practical arts as cooking, maternity care, sewing, were held for members. The Liga at times gives help to African elites in trouble with their governments. The case of Eduardo Daniel, a schoolteacher, is an example. Daniel in 1954 was expelled from the Huambo district by the Bailundu administrator as an undesirable character. He appealed to the governor-general and was called to Luanda. While there, Daniel requested aid from the Liga. Officers and members offered him legal and financial help. The governor-general reviewed his case but sustained the Bailundu administrator's action. Eduardo Daniel was sent to the penal colony at Baia dos Tigres for three years. After a year he was allowed to live in Moçamedes, a port city. Two years later Daniel returned to his home in Bailundu. Africans in central Angola appreciated the financial and legal aid the Liga gave to Eduardo Daniel.

Close ties with the government have hindered the Liga's freedom to act. An annual government grant is made by the governor-general to the Liga from his contingency fund. Recently leaders of the Liga Africana have attempted to dissociate themselves from the government's policy in Angola. One group wrote a manifesto in 1956 in the hope that it could be presented to the United Nations. The manifesto hoped to draw attention to the plight of the Africans in Angola. Pressure on the Liga by the government for support of their African policy has increased. In 1957 the directors were requested by the governor-general to send a delegation to the United Nations to corroborate Portugal's claim that Angola is an integral province of the mother country. Portugal wanted to be exempt from making the report on her African possessions which is required in regard to non-self-governing territories. The directors of the Liga declined. The refusal led to an overhaul of the Liga's organization and new directors were chosen by the governor-general.

The Liga Africana is the only legal secular African organization in Angola, appealing to the educated elites. Political organizations other than the government party, União Nacional, are illegal. No voluntary group can be formed without the approval of the governor-general. To be certified, the group must submit its constitution to the governor-general's office, specifying its aims, the names of its directors and its locality. Control is absolute. Opposition to the government must go underground, and punishment is severe for those who are caught. Fifteen years of imprisonment is not an unusual sentence for a political prisoner.

Voluntary African interest groups in the field of sports and in religion do exist. Luanda, Benguela and Nova Lisboa sponsor all-African soccer (futebul) leagues. The best African players are invited to join European clubs. Often feelings of national solidarity are expressed in support of an African player. Matateu, an African from Mozambique, is an example. He is the hero of all African schoolchildren. Matateu, in the field of sports, is the symbol of African superiority.

Many religious youth groups are sponsored by Catholic and Protestant bodies. District councils and parishes encourage regional youth meetings. A step in this direction was the first Angola Christian Youth Congress held in 1955. Two years later a second congress was called. Often a local youth group is censured by the government because of its activities. Such was the case with the

*Avante* group in the district of Bié. *Avante* means "progress," and government authorities were suspicious of the aims of such a group. Africans interpreted *avante* in terms of cultural self-improvement, but the government saw *avante* as the vanguard of a political movement.

In spite of the government's order banning political groups, there are signs that some exist in Angola. The arrest by PIDE of four Africans in 1957 for acts against the "security of the State" called attention to this fact. PIDE determined to stamp out these groups, and in March 1959, PIDE arrested twenty-eight Africans. The names of the arrested persons were published in the newspapers. Who are these Africans, and how well organized are they?

The occupations of the twenty-eight Africans varied. The list included two mechanics, twelve civil service employees, eight nurses, a clerk, a teacher, a student, a printer, a Catholic priest and a writer. The political activities of the group centered in Luanda. They served primarily as an information group. The impetus of these movements came from political exiles. Twelve names were mentioned besides the twenty-eight arrested. Two lived in Matadi; five in Leopoldville; two in Paris; one each in Brazzaville and Brazil. An American seaman, George Barnett, was also implicated. All were connected with one of the five organized groups in exile set up for the purpose of liberating the peoples of Portuguese Africa:

> Movimento Popular de Libertação de Angola
> Partido Africano de Independência de Guiné
> Movimento Para a Independência Nacional de Angola
> Movimento Anti-Colonista
> União das Populações de Angola

At the second All-African People's Congress, held in Tunis in 1960, the first four of these organizations combined to form the *Frente Revolucionária Africana para a Independência das Colónias Portuguesas* (FRAIN), with headquarters in Conakry, Republic of Guinea. The fifth organization, *União das Populações de Angola*, operates out of Leopoldville, Republic of Congo. The leaders of these organizations are on the Portuguese list of "undesirables" and are in exile. Mário Coelho Pinto de Andrade, member of FRAIN, is listed as a resident of Paris and associated with a group called

Présence Africaine. João Cabral lives in England as the London representative of Movimento Popular de Libertação de Angola. Alvaro Holden Roberto, secretary of União das Populações de Angola, lives in Leopoldville. Holden Roberto is best known to the Africans in Angola, and is one of the seven who founded the UPA as the first national party in 1954.

These five organizations seek independence from Portugal. They reject the arguments that Angola, Mozambique, Portuguese Guinea, São Tomé, Cabo Verdes and Príncipe belong to the Portuguese, for a number of reasons. For one thing, the concept of Portugal's historical rights has never been accepted by Africans; they regard the Portuguese as conquerors, not as a people belonging to Africa. Another consideration is that Portugal herself is an underdeveloped country. The average weekly earnings of Portuguese industrial workers in 1958 were $5.24. Dr. K. K. Rao of the Food and Agricultural Organization's Nutrition Division reported that in 1954-1955 the "intake of calories by the Portuguese people was the lowest in Europe, and was equal to the intake in Tunisia and the then Belgian Congo." [7] Furthermore, Portugal's per capita gross national product is only slightly higher than that of Ghana, a country which has not as yet been able to solve its own problems.[8] Africans, therefore, question the ability of the Portuguese to develop her overseas territories. Next, the policy of assimilation is unacceptable not only in theory but even more in practice. It is based on the racist idea of the incompetence of African people, and implies that African cultures have no value. Also, the fundamental rights of man as defined by the Universal Declaration of December 10, 1948 —freedom of speech, of the press, of religion and of association— are violated by existing fascist laws in Angola. Finally, the claim of national unity is a subterfuge which contradicts all geographic, historical, ethnic, social and cultural facts.

As of 1961, the five organizations have done little more than hold discussions among the elite, and publish and distribute pamphlets and leaflets. Within Angola their appeal has been to all segments of the population. They call attention to the feats of the women of Ghana, Guinea, Cameroons, Togo, Congo and Somaliland during those countries' campaigns for independence, and exhort the women in Angola to do likewise. To the tribal chiefs, they say:

"Certain members of your group have become instruments of colonialism. They have permitted the recruitment of forced labourers and have supported the policy of heavy taxation, and in a great portion of Angola their position has made them traitors. You must fully realize that the moment has come for you to make your choice between your country, your sons, your brothers on the one hand, and the colonists on the other." [9]

The demands upon youth are heavy. It is to them that the elders look for new values, values which will make Angola's voice heard immediately in the concert of nations. They must stand ready to come to the aid of all who are working for national liberation. They enjoin the Portuguese colonists to participate in the struggle, though they recognize that some have amassed enormous fortunes at the expense of African labor. To them they say that the hour has come when restitution must be made to the Angolans for their land and resources. As for the others, they invite them to remain in Angola so that together they can work for the establishment of an Angolan Republic, democratic and socially just.

Internationally, they appeal for help from all African peoples and from such worldwide organizations as the United Nations. To the African peoples they say: "No African can remain indifferent to the existence of colonialism on our continent. Each one of us has a definite duty to perform: To liquidate the colonial regime, the colonialist spirit, the colonial ideal." [10] They call upon all international organizations to bring pressures to bear upon Portugal so that the regime of exploitation in Angola shall cease and the territory recover its independence of ancient days.

How do these groups hope to achieve their ends? The UPA claims a membership of 40,000, including Angolans who are living in the Congo. It publishes a newspaper, *The Voice of the Angolan Nation*, whose circulation is reported as 20,000. The newspaper is published in four languages—French, Portuguese, Kikongo and Kimbundu. Since its founding in 1954, the UPA has enlisted the help of the existing Bakongo party. This is understandable, because there are 500,000 Kikongo-speaking peoples in the Portuguese Congo. It is significant that the site of the Bakongo kingdom was in the Portuguese Congo, São Salvador. Patrice Lumumba, when premier of the Congo, and President Kasavubu publicly announced that they would work for the reestablishment of the unity of the Bakongo peoples. Neither indicated how he would accomplish this.

The Frente Revolucionária Africana para a Independência das Colónias Portuguesas, on the other hand, is closely tied to the Republics of Guinea, Ghana and Mali. Its mode of operation is parallel to the pattern already established in those countries. Its concern is for the liberation of all Portuguese Africa, while the Leopoldville-based UPA is more oriented toward Angola.

## Portuguese Security Measures

The Portuguese know of the existence of FRAIN and UPA. They are aware of the development of nationalism and consider it a menace. The armed forces in Angola have always backed the Portuguese government. In 1956 the army had 279 commissioned and 374 noncommissioned officers—all Europeans. Of the 5,831 enlisted men, 399 were Europeans and 5,435 were Africans. The marines had 11 commisioned and 14 noncommissioned officers, all Europeans. Of the 153 enlisted men, 20 were Europeans.[11]

Recent events indicate a strengthening of the military forces in Angola. The governor-general of Angola, at a ceremony in March 1959 inaugurating the shooting range in Luanda, said:

The instruction to shoot is one of the most important things for the soldier. The events which are running in neighboring territories are not clear nor comforting and it is precisely because of this that all brave men in our Province are responsible and ready. It is necessary to know how to use arms for the day which may arrive. We must not be unaware as to what is going on around us. A man forewarned is worth two. . . . Portuguese troops must be trained to shoot with greater efficiency; otherwise lack of preparedness will be interpreted as a sign of weakness by the newly created independent African nations.[12]

On this occasion also the governor-general announced that within a few weeks there would be installed two divisions of armed

units, a naval craft and an air force unit. This was substantiated by
the London *Times* of May 27, 1960, reporting

altogether, probably, about 2,000 metropolitan troops have been brought
into Angola in the past year or 18 months, contributing to a total of
nearly 20,000 soldiers. Although the majority of these are African, the
hard core of the metropolitan regulars is assisted by some 3,000 or 4,000
Angolan whites, who do their two years compulsory Portuguese military
training in their home territory. The army is equipped with newly arrived Banhard armoured cars, quick-firing guns, and troop transporters,
and in the bush 10 miles outside Luanda a large military enclosure has
been built recently, for storing new equipment. In five of the towns
visited, from São António do Zaire, at the mouth of the Congo to Moçamedes on the fringe of the Kalahari desert your correspondent saw
new barrack buildings. At Nova Lisboa, on the Benguela railway which
leads into the Belgian Congo, the new barracks hold 3,000 men, and
some of the others were obviously built for more troops that were said
to be occupying them at the time. Two small motor gunboats have been
patrolling the Angola coast occasionally for the past year. Military air-
craft are expected to be based in Angola for the first time this summer,
and a new airfield is being prepared for them at Tolo in the Portuguese
Congo.[13]

The large number of enlisted Africans is of great concern to
the Portuguese government. Military authorities ask themselves:
Can they count on the loyalty of the African enlisted men in time
of internal crisis? Is the training given to African soldiers in the use
of modern arms a wise policy? The Portuguese command deploys
recruited men from one area to another, sends recruits from the south
of Angola to the northern section which borders the Republic of
Congo, to keep the African soldiers from identifying with the village
peoples. Incidents that demonstrate the hostility of the Congolese
to the invaders from the south are frequently reported. Playing off
one tribe against another is a centuries-old technique employed by
the colonial powers in Africa. Africans are also reminded that the
Portuguese army is European controlled. Early in 1959 a display
of Portugal's might was shown in Luanda by a demonstration of
parachute troops and napalm bombs.
    Besides the buildup of military forces, the government has
called upon its security police, PIDE, to maintain order within

Angola. Police actions in 1956 alone were taken against 2,931 crimes.

### XI. CRIMES AGAINST WHICH POLICE ACTIONS WERE TAKEN IN 1956[14]

|                                        | Male  | Female | Total |
|----------------------------------------|-------|--------|-------|
| Crimes against public order and tranquility | 989   | 62     | 1,051 |
| Crimes against persons                 | 795   | 45     | 840   |
| Crimes against property                | 1,015 | 25     | 1,040 |
|                                        | 2,799 | 132    | 2,931 |

Crimes against public order seem excessive in proportion to the other two categories of crimes—against persons and against property. In Portugal, reports show that "between March and July 1960, 103 people were tried on political charges, and were sentenced to a total of 138 years in prison, loss of political rights for a total of 725 years, and security measures, that is, the prolongation of prison terms by the political police, which can transform any prison term into a life sentence—totalling 123 years." [15]

In Angola, Europeans have always dominated the police. In 1956 there were 313 Europeans and 151 Africans in this security branch.[16] The police have been growing in importance. Their handling of the political prisoners in 1960 and the expulsion of the executive secretary of the Evangelical Alliance in March 1960 showed the efficiency of their methods of investigation. They lie beyond the scope and control of the civil administration. Their authority is even greater than that of the governor-general with respect to "crimes against the State." The Portuguese constitution gives PIDE authority to imprison political prisoners without formal charges. Foreigners can be held for thirty days without any charges and Portuguese citizens for sixty days. There is no resort once PIDE acts, and no one can question its actions.

PIDE and the Portuguese armed forces will not hesitate to use arms to quell a rebellion. The killing of thirty-one people in the February 6, 1961, Luanda riots is a good example. The outlook for the future is dark: more riots and more killings. The Portuguese are determined to stay in Angola until the "bitter end."

# 5. PORTUGAL UNDER FIRE

## In the United Nations

Afro-Asian nations are stepping up their criticisms of Portugal and her colonial policies in Africa. The United Nations is being used as the arena. Because of these attacks, high government officials in Portugal question the advisability of continuing her membership in the UN.

The reason Portugal is a member of the United Nations is because she is a member of NATO. When Portugal signed the North Atlantic Treaty in 1949, Portugal's allies urged her to apply for membership in the United Nations. On July 11, 1949, the United States ambassador to the UN, Warren R. Austin, supported Portugal's application before the Security Council. On September 13, 1949, Portugal with six other applicants—Jordan, Italy, Finland, Ireland, Austria, and Ceylon—received a majority vote in the UN Security Council, but the negative vote by the U.S.S.R. blocked their admission. On November 22, 1949, the General Assembly considered the application of Portugal for United Nations membership and passed a resolution that Portugal is in its judgment a peace-loving state within the meaning of Article 4 of the Charter and is able and willing to carry out the obligations of the Charter and therefore should be admitted to membership in the UN. The Security Council was asked to reconsider the application of Portugal in the light of this determination of the General Assembly.[1] It was not until December 14, 1955, however, that Portugal, with sixteen other nations, was voted into the United Nations.

Portugal is not an enthusiastic member of the United Nations. Portugal's presence in that organization has given member nations

the opportunity to attack her colonial policies. The representative of
Portugal reporting from the eleventh General Assembly to his
country stated that in the Commission for Social, Cultural and
Humanitarian Problems, there was a vigorous attack on colonialism
led by Russia with the collaboration of Uruguay, Greece, Syria,
Rumania, Guatemala, Arabia, Egypt, Burma, Indonesia, Haiti and
Afghanistan. He pointed out two things: that the accusations of
colonialism will not stop but will continue to preoccupy the United
Nations, and that the number of votes against colonialism will increase in the coming years, with the independence of more Afro-Asian
countries.[2] He was proved correct by the events in the 1960-1961
General Assembly of the United Nations.

Article 73e of the UN Charter, the declaration regarding non-
self-governing territories, has provided the grounds on which Portugal
has been attacked by member nations. This section states:

> Members of the United Nations which have or assumed responsi-
> bilities for the administration of territories whose peoples have not yet
> attained a full measure of self-government must transmit regularly to
> the Secretary General for information purposes, subject to such limitation
> as security and constitutional considerations may require, statistical and
> other information of a technical nature relating to economic, social, and
> educational conditions in the territories for which they are respectively
> responsible other than those territories to which Chapters XII and XIII
> apply.[3]

The Assembly in 1959 appointed a special committee to implement this charter provision, and one of the most important of the
principles which were drawn up by the committee states that "there
is an obligation to transmit information in respect of a territory which
is geographically separate and is distinct ethnically and/or culturally
from the country administering it." [4] The draft resolution endorsing
the principles was adopted by the Fourth Committee by 62 votes to
3 (Portugal, Spain and the Union of South Africa), with 19 abstentions. The proposal of the Fourth Committee goes on to declare
that "an obligation exists on the part of the government of Portugal
to supply such information" and that this obligation "should be
discharged without further delay." The resolution declares further
that "the desire for independence is the rightful aspiration of

peoples under colonial subjugation and that the denial of their right to self-determination constitutes a threat to the well-being of humanity and a threat to international peace." The draft resolution lists Angola as the largest of the Portuguese territories.

During the eleven-day debate which followed the committee's action, "differences arose concerning the status of certain territories administered by Spain and Portugal and the obligations of the two countries to submit data to the United Nations on those territories in accordance with the provisions of Article 73 of the Charter. With a view to resolving such differences, the General Assembly in 1959 created a Special Committee of Six charged with studying the principles which should guide members in determining whether or not an obligation exists to transmit the information called for in Article 73e." [5]

The Committee of Six, prefacing the list of principles, stated: "The right of dependent peoples to choose their own destiny is more universally accepted today than at any time since the signing of the Charter in San Francisco. . . . There now exists general recognition that independence is among the rightful aspirations of every nation, the fulfillment of which is an important factor in the preservation of international peace and security. The Charter is a living document, and the obligations under Chapter XI must be viewed in the light of the changing spirit of the times." [6]

In the debate which followed, Portugal's representative, Alberto Franco Nogueira, once again reminded the Assembly that the territories involved are overseas provinces of the homeland and as such do not come within the scope of the Charter's provisions regarding non-self-governing territories. Mr. Nogueira argued as follows:

In what context should Article 73 and Chapter XI be read? The obvious answer was that they should be read in the context of the Charter. The Charter established three different systems for the promotion of the welfare of peoples and for cooperation among nations in the social, economic, educational, and political fields. The first system was that provided by Chapters IX and X of the Charter, entitled "International Economic and Social Cooperation"; the second was that outlined in Chapter XI entitled "Declaration Regarding Non-Self-Governing Territories"; the third was laid down in Chapter XII entitled "International Trusteeship System." The first and third were "International" systems. In other words, the authors of the Charter, by placing them under the

heading, had intended that the international community, through the
appropriate machinery of the United Nations, should have a say in their
implementation. As for the second system, the word "international" had
been omitted, which was an indication that the problem was considered
to be national rather than international in character.[7]

The representative of Portugal also pointed out that transmis-
sion of information arising from security and constitutional considerations poses limitations on the interpretation of Article 73e. Mr.
Nogueira affirmed that

they alone had to determine, in accordance with their own constitution,
the limitations which might exist. The interpretation of a national constitution was a matter within the exclusive competence of a member state
and was not one for discussion by any international body; a dangerous
precedent would be set by acting otherwise. Constitutional limitations
operated in two ways: they could limit the nature or amount of the information provided, in cases where a government was allowed to transmit information, and they could prohibit a member state from supplying
information on territories and populations whose political status that
state alone could define.[8]

Many speakers rebutted Portugal's legal arguments on the
interpretation of Article 73e. Mr. Krishna Menon stated that "it had
become impossible to speak of colonies from a purely legal point of
view. The Charter prescribed respect for human rights and the
maintenance of international peace and security. It imposed on the
Portuguese government the obligation at least to transmit information
on the economic, social, and educational conditions in the territories
it administered." [9]

After further discussion, the committee adopted by 45 votes to 5,
with 24 abstentions, the draft resolution as a whole. Member nations
who voted against the draft resolution were: Belgium, Brazil, Portugal, Spain and the Union of South Africa. Members casting an
abstention ballot were: Albania, Australia, Austria, Bulgaria, Byelorus-
sian S.S.R., Canada, Chile, China, Colombia, Czechoslovakia,
Dominican Republic, Hungary, Italy, Japan, Netherlands, New
Zealand, Pakistan, Panama, Poland, Romania, Ukrainian S.S.R.,
U.S.S.R., United Kingdom and United States.

Reactions in Portugal against the United Nations resolution were bitter. The criticism produced a wave of nationalistic fervor. Pro-Salazar rallies were held throughout the country. On October 19, 1960, thousands of students in Lisbon gathered in front of the office of the Minister of National Education protesting the accusations against Portugal in the UN. Students of all grades—elementary, high school and university—were present. Libertário Viegas, a student in his third year in the Science Faculty, promised that the youth delegations of Lisbon (comprised of representatives from all the provinces of Portugal) pledged their solidarity in the position of Portugal in Africa. Another student, Pedro Ortet, born in Guinea and a first-year law student, affirmed that Portugal has governed well in Portuguese Africa. He said:

> We are well governed because we live in peace and progress. Portugal gives us a reason to live. She has lifted us up from an obscure and inconsequential civilization and has integrated us completely into a more experienced culture. The lesson of the Congo is not lost on us. If the peace which is promised to us and if the liberty which is offered to us are similar to that of the Congo, we have to confess that they do not entice us. . . . We affirm once again that the youth are ready to defend the interest of the nation and to shed their blood if it is necessary that Portuguese Africa continue to be an integral part of Portugal.[10]

Dr. Salazar addressed the National Assembly on November 30, 1960, and scored his critics for "abusive intervention by third parties in our internal affairs." He further stated that "Portugal had no intention of equating her overseas provinces with United Nations trusteeship territories. That was the basis on which we were admitted to the United Nations," he said. "Had it been otherwise, we would never have joined." [11]

Government rallies protesting the United Nations resolution were also organized in Angola. Residents proclaimed their loyalty to the Salazar government. Africans and mulattoes were prominently displayed on the speaker's platform. In the city of Silva Porto, the crowd applauded António José Maria, an African, and Emídio da Fonseca Santo, a mulatto, for their manifestation of loyalty to Portugal. The governor of the district, Manuel Henriques de Carvalho, concluded the rally with these words: "Here is Portugal. And

Portugal cannot be separated because it is One Nation, united and indivisible. We do not agree that strangers interfere with our problems. We do not have colonies. The overseas territories are provinces of Portugal just as Algarve, Minho, or Beira." [12]

African leaders reject Portugal's defense. In the debate on the Assembly's resolution, Joseph Adam Braimah of Ghana spoke these words: "In order to become an *assimilado* an African in Angola or Mozambique is expected to adopt a European mode of life, abandon African ways of living and invariably come around to professing the Christian religion. A mere decree cannot transmute Africans into Portuguese. Portugal must come to terms with reality and take fully into account the aspirations of these people for independence." [13]

Speaking for Nigeria, Nuhu Bamali said: "Angola and Mozambique are both geographically and ethnically separated from Portugal. Their people do not enjoy the same rights as the Portuguese people and fewer than 0.1 per cent of the indigenous inhabitants of the two territories are Portuguese." [14] Miss Angie Brooks of Liberia warned the Assembly that it had no choice but to request Portugal to implement the obligations it undertook in joining the United Nations. "The Assembly should recommend that Portugal advance with the tide of history and see that the territories under its administration and the peoples under its rule in Africa and Asia are delivered from Portuguese administration and that they join the community of free nations." [15]

The continued attacks by African and Asian delegates have indeed raised doubts in official Portuguese circles of the value of continued membership in the United Nations. Western observers in Lisbon predict that in the future Portugal will boycott further debates on her overseas provinces.


## In the United States


The position of the United States in this conflict is important, since the political and economic ties between Portugal and the United States have great bearing on the future status of Angola.

The signing of the North Atlantic Treaty in Washington on April 4, 1949, marked the first step into closer military cooperation between the two countries. This treaty makes clear that all the parties to it will come to the defense should an armed attack occur against any of them. In accordance with the aim of the treaty, the Azores Defense Agreement was signed by the United States and Portugal on September 6, 1951. The meeting in Lisbon in February 1952 of all members of the North Atlantic Treaty brought to the attention of the world that Portugal had allied herself with the West.

Since the mid-fifties the United States has forged closer and closer ties with the Salazar regime in Portugal. Secretary of State Dulles on November 30, 1955, invited the Portuguese Foreign Minister, Dr. Paulo Cunha, to the United States for a state visit. Twelve days later in a press conference, Secretary Dulles, queried on the United States position in regard to the status of Goa, said: "All the world regards Goa as a Portuguese province. I do not think there is any particular controversy about the status of these areas under the constitution of Portugal." President Eisenhower, after the collapse of the summit conference in May 1960, visited Lisbon and gave his blessings to the Salazar government. He said:

My talks with President Tomás and with the President of the Council, Dr. Salazar, have been conducted in a spirit of complete mutual understanding. All of us realize that we are united in a common cause and that each of us, in his own way, shares a part of the responsibility of striving for a peaceful and better world. Moreover, our talks together have once again affirmed the spirit of friendship and good will that has always characterized the relations between Portugal and the United States.[16]

Other treaty agreements have brought the two nations closer together. A bilateral agreement in connection with the European Recovery Program was signed on September 28, 1948, at Lisbon by Ambassador MacVeagh of the United States and the Portuguese Foreign Minister. On May 27, 1956, both countries signed an agreement on surplus agricultural commodities; and on July 21, 1955, the United States and Portugal concluded an agreement for cooperation concerning civil uses of atomic energy.

Meanwhile, trade with the United States has become an important factor in the economy of Angola. During the period 1938-1942 the United States ranked third in volume of trade in the list of Angola's foreign markets; in 1943-1947 the United States climbed to first place, with 9.5 per cent of the trade volume; this increased to 14.8 per cent in the period 1948-1952. Furthermore, Dr. José Nunes de Oliveira, former governor-general of Mozambique and inspector-general of overseas administration, stated in his address to the North American Assembly on African Affairs, held in Ohio in June 1952, that the United States contributed a substantial sum to Portugal's development program of 600,000,000 escudos for Angolan harbors, railways, hydroelectric power plants, urbanization projects and medical and educational welfare programs for Africans. The amount of the U.S. contribution was not specified.

United States capital continues to buttress the Angolan and Portuguese economies. In 1961 the Gulf Oil Company engaged in explorations in Cabinda on the enclave of the Congo River. The announcement, in January 1961, of the multination bond issue of $10,000,000 of a large Portuguese company, the Sociedade Anónima Concessionária de Refinação de Petróleos em Portugal, involved further United States capital. Underwriters received orders for the bonds from the United States, Britain, France, Belgium, Luxembourg, the Netherlands, Switzerland and West Germany. The amount of United States capital invested in the bond issue is not known. It is significant, however, that the counsel for the underwriters was the Paris office of the American law firm of Cleary, Gottlieb, Steen and Ball.[17]

The political and economic ties of the United States and Portugal have raised doubts in the minds of Africans about the position of the United States on the question of Portuguese Africa. What do the Africans hope from the United States? They would like to see the United States insist that arms given Portugal under NATO not be used directly or indirectly against Africans in Portuguese Africa. African leaders recognize that NATO is an organization built to defend the freedom of Europe. But they cannot accept NATO's use against freedom in Africa, and they blame the United States for not controlling the ultimate destination and effects of military aid to Europe. Again, African leaders hope that the United States will give full backing to the moves by the African group at the United Nations to make Portugal account for her actions in Africa and introduce reform there. They say Portugal's claim that her overseas territories are domestic affairs is ludicrous.

The episode of the *Santa Maria* raised the hopes of many that the United States had reappraised her policy towards Portugal. When the *Santa Maria* was seized by Captain Henrique Galvão and his men, the United States Navy, in response to Portugal's appeal for help, mobilized ships and planes to search for the ship. Within the next twenty-four hours, the United States government retreated from its original assessment of the seizure as an act of "piracy." The news of the change in the United States view was received with great displeasure in Lisbon. "The machine guns, false passports, and grenades were paid for with Communist funds," an official declared. "Portugal's allies have got to face squarely up to the international implications of the situation. The great powers cannot wash their hands of the affair like Pontius Pilate." [18]

Further complications were avoided when the vessel docked at the Brazilian port of Recife. The passengers landed safely and the *Santa Maria* returned to the Portuguese government. In Lisbon, even the United States Navy, whose handling of the search and surveillance operations had been criticized sharply here earlier, received a share of praise. "The United States Navy has done much, a great deal," the government's official spokesman, Ramiro Valdez of the Information Department, said on February 3. Senhor Valdez added that the government had never criticized the American efforts or made a protest to Washington.[19]

The incident of the *Santa Maria* accomplished one thing: it made the United States reappraise her position in regard to Portuguese Africa. The *New York Times* editorial of February 11, 1961, entitled "The Trouble With Angola," expressed this reappraisal:

Colonialism and racism are two features of contemporary life whose end is in sight. Where they persist unchanged, it is because of a refusal to recognize realities. No people are being more stubborn in rejecting the facts of twentieth-century life than the present rulers of Portugal. . . . The Portuguese are defying all the rules of logic by calling Angola and Mozambique integral parts of Portuguese national territory and therefore not colonies. Anything is possible when you do your own defining. . . . This is no longer a world where the black man, because he is black, can be held in virtual servitude and in ignorance and disease.[20]

The support by the United States of the Liberian resolution in the Security Council on March 15, 1961, was another evidence of a shift in American policy. Liberia's resolution called for reform in Angola, progress toward independence, and a UN Commission of inquiry into conditions in Angola. Five nations voted for the resolution—the United States, U.S.S.R., Liberia, Ceylon and the United Arab Republic. Six abstained—Britain, France, Turkey, Nationalist China, Ecuador and Chile. The resolution failed to pass the Security Council by two votes. Afro-Asian delegates to the United Nations welcomed the shift in United States policy. They were delighted to hear the United States Ambassador to the United Nations, Adlai Stevenson, say that the important thing was to insure that similar conditions which exist in the former Belgian Congo do not exist in Angola. Therefore, he continued, the best course of action to promote the interests of the people of Portuguese territories seemed to be through cooperation with the United Nations.[21] Needless to say, Portugal did not appreciate Mr. Stevenson's admonitions. The government newspaper, *Diário da Manha*, scored the United States vote as "an act of stupidity" that she would repent.[22]

The United States occupies an unenviable position: whatever she does, she will be damned. Africans say, however, that the United States must abide by her decision of March 15, 1961. There is no escape. A shift of policy will cost the United States the good will of the Africans in Angola and the good will of the 25 per cent of the membership of the United Nations which is African. Whether the United States wants it or not, Angola will be free. The United States has most to lose if she reverses her March 15 policy.

# 6. THE OUTBREAK OF VIOLENCE IN ANGOLA

March 1961 marked the beginning of open civil war in Angola. *O Comercio*, a newspaper published in Luanda, reported in its April 12 issue the existing state of war. The headline read: "It is necessary to act, considering that we are actually at war." [1] The quoted words were taken from a speech given in the Portuguese National Assembly by the deputy, Captain Silva Mendes. The speaker declared that the only way to defeat the insurrectionists was through military power.

The acts of violence perpetrated by Africans and Portuguese raise the question: Who is to blame? Official Portuguese dispatches held that the rebellion was planned and executed by foreign agitators—probably from the Republic of Congo. They cite instances in which captured Africans spoke neither Portuguese nor the African languages of the area, Kikongo or Kimbundu. The Portuguese are convinced that the core of the insurgents is Communist. They blame the Conakry-based Angolan exiles and the UPA in Leopoldville for stirring up the rebellion. Both are accused of being leftist-oriented. Furthermore, military authorities in Angola say that African prisoners admit being in contact with the Congolese left-wing party, the Party of African Solidarity under the presidency of Antoine Gizenga.

The leader of the UPA party, Holden Roberto, denies the Portuguese accusations that the March disturbances are the work of outside organizers. The Angolan, in an interview with newspaper reporters in Leopoldville, described the incidents as spontaneous uprisings touched off when the manager of a forced labor farm, Primavera, located near the town of São Salvador, opened fire because his workers were demanding higher wages and better living conditions. In retaliation the workers attacked the manager with their

81

shovels and machetes, and killed him. The unrest spread to neighboring farms. Other Portuguese supervisors fired on the workers and a general state of unrest followed. When Portuguese military units rushed in to defend the white settlers, the workers fled into the forests to wage a guerrilla war.

Portuguese reaction to the rebellion was: "Let's kill the stupid *pretos* (blacks)." For this purpose every white settler was offered arms, not only to defend himself from surprise attacks, but to kill indiscriminately any potentially dangerous African in his neighborhood. Civilian defense corps patrolled African quarters and foreign institutions such as Protestant missions. Portuguese vigilantes in Luanda sponsored night raids on defenseless Africans, killing many suspected sympathizers of the Angolan nationalist movements in exile.

In Portugal, Premier Salazar dismissed his defense minister and took over the Defense Ministry. The dismissed minister, General Júlio Botelho Moniz, was reported to have headed a group of high ranking officers who demanded changes in Portugal's overseas policies. Other dismissals included the army and overseas ministers, the defense chief of staff and the military governor of Lisbon. Premier Salazar's first move as defense minister was to order all Portuguese security and armed forces to stand by in a "state of prevention." This also included the sending of troop reinforcements to Angola. Paratroopers numbering between 2,500 and 3,000 were immediately flown to Luanda, the Angolan capital. On May 5, 1961, approximately 3,400 troops sailed aboard the liner *Vera Cruz* for Angola. Arms and equipment were shipped on the *Rita Maria*. Portuguese troops continue to pour into Angola to bolster the government's campaign to crush the revolt in northern Angola. Reports indicate that about 15,000 to 18,000 Portuguese troops are engaged in the war.

To bolster his position Premier Salazar made further changes in his cabinet. On May 3 new Ministers of Interior, Foreign Affairs, Education and Corporation and Social Insurance were appointed. A new Secretary of State for Commerce, Industry and Agriculture and a new Under-Secretary for Education were also chosen by Salazar. The cabinet shifts indicated no change in Portugal's overseas policy. The new Overseas Minister, Adriano Moreira, on arriving in Luanda on May 1, 1961, said, "My presence here confirms the firm decision of the government to use all necessary means to bring back peace and security to Angola and to keep her Portuguese." [2]

The policy to keep Angola Portuguese has meant first, waves of arrests in the towns bordering Luanda and in the capital itself. All Africans classified by the secret police, PIDE, as sympathizers of African nationalism have been arrested. Those detained are the educated elites, and they face long periods of imprisonment without due process or trial. Second, Portuguese armed forces are engaging in a policy of extermination as they battle the nationalist forces in the north. Angolan refugees in the Congo, mainly from the Bakongo tribe, relate incidents of bombings and mass killings by Portuguese troops. Over 60,000 Africans are reported to have fled across the border into the Congo because of fear of reprisals by the Portuguese.

The continued resistance by Africans has forced the Portuguese to resort to military actions rather than other programs. On March 20, 1961, rumors from Lisbon indicated that constitutional changes were being prepared for Angola. The new proposals hinted at greater autonomy for the overseas provinces. A month later, however, the Portuguese government decided to postpone the proposed plans for constitutional changes. Instead, stricter government controls were placed upon Africans. The government prohibited public gatherings, religious or secular; established roadblocks at every government post, which effectively checked car movements; and restricted Africans to the area of their own villages. Martial law placed control of northern Angola in the hands of the military powers.

In Portugal itself, meanwhile, there has been mounting criticism of Premier Salazar's colonial policy. Professional men—lawyers, journalists, professors, doctors, engineers, artists and writers—called on the government to restore democratic liberties in Portugal and renounce any colonial imperialism. The program further advocated an improvement in the standard of living and education of Africans and job opportunities for all without racial discrimination, including high government posts for Africans. The government rejected the proposals and replied that it was all the more regrettable for the opposition to present them when the nation was engaged in reestablishing order in Angola and perturbed by cruel acts of terrorism organized beyond its frontiers. The government scored the opposition, saying that the energy expended by them could better be used in the defense of the Angolan people who already have made large sacrifices.[3]

If the opposition grows, Portugal will face trouble on two fronts —at home and in her overseas possessions. There is a definite move to extend the trouble spots. Goan nationalists are redoubling their efforts to liberate their country from Portuguese rule. Will Mozambique and Portuguese Guinea also come into the act? The conference of nationalists from Portuguese Africa, meeting at Morocco in April 1961, indicated some such strategy. Portugal is indeed in trouble.

### Factors in Angola Violence

Benjamin Welles, *New York Times* correspondent, in analyzing the violence in Angola, has mentioned three points:

First, there is overwhelming evidence that the attacks were organized and led by foreign African revolutionaries and timed to foreign events such as a United Nations discussion of Angola. Second, Africans of Angola in surprising numbers joined in the revolts against Portuguese authority, either because of economic distress or discontent over harsh controls or both. Third, the so-called Portuguese multiracial society of whites, mulattoes and Africans living in a classless society is being threatened by the white Portuguese immigrants whom the regime of Premier Salazar is sending out in growing numbers. This clash is unabashedly dedicated to white supremacy, and is already weighing a future bloc composed of an independent white-ruled Angola allied to the white-ruled Union of South Africa and Southern Rhodesia.[4]

To substantiate his first point that the revolt is led and directed by foreigners, Mr. Welles referred to the capture of seventy-one Ghanaians by the Portuguese on May 11. But Africans reject Mr. Welles's analysis for these reasons: (1) The rebellion is an indigenous movement; the leaders may be in exile, but they are Angolans by birth. (2) Africans consider Angola as their problem. The conference of twenty independent African states held in Liberia in May 1961 passed a resolution acknowledging that the question of Angola is an African problem; they identify themselves with Angolan nationalists in their struggle against the Portuguese. To Africans, the Portuguese are the foreigners who are holding on to their position as conquerors. Because the Portuguese have greater military power, Angolan nationalists are appealing for help from their kinsmen in other parts of Africa. (3) It would indeed be strange for Africans in northern Angola not to have been involved in such an organized rebellion as pictured by Benjamin Welles. Food, shelter, guides, communication are necessary elements of any revolution. This could only have been accomplished through cooperation with the villagers. Portuguese authorities have always been naive in believing that Africans in Angola are not capable of organizing and leading an independence movement. No one would question, however, the involvement of African nationalists from outside Angola in the struggle to free Angola from Portuguese control. But we must remember that the brunt of the battle is borne by Angolan Africans—in organization, leadership and participation.

A much more basic question in analyzing the Angolan violence is: Why fight now? And, what do the Angolan nationalists hope to accomplish? It is difficult to determine the reasons why Africans rebelled in northern Angola at this particular time. Was it a planned strategy? Or was it a spontaneous reaction to a particular economic situation—as Holden Roberto suggests in his analysis—the demand of workers at the Primavera farm for higher wages and better living conditions? Reports indicate that both Portuguese and Angolan nationalists were surprised at the sudden and violent acts of rebellion. However, when the fire was ignited, Africans put into force plans they had readied for just such an eventuality. This is substantiated in later reports, showing more advanced revolutionary techniques. Bands wielding such primitive equipment as machetes were replaced by units employing automatic weapons and petrol bombs. Modern arms will be more accessible to the Africans as the war progresses, especially if the Congo government carries out its promise to link all the Bakongo speaking peoples into a single ethnic group.

Tactically, the war will be prolonged, since the wooded and

grassy hill terrain is ideal for guerrilla warfare. Communications can also be disrupted by Africans, isolating European communities. The Portuguese would be safe only in large towns, such as Carmona and Salazar. Furthermore, the conditions of guerrilla warfare necessitate living off the land. Africans can do this; Portuguese soldiers cannot. This fact may tip the balance in favor of the Africans unless the Portuguese successfully exterminate the nationalists in northern Angola through bombings, strafing, and the use of armored tanks. Even if the Portuguese subdued the nationalists, they will still face the problem of patrolling the 480 miles of Congo boundary. Continued harrassment at all points by African guerrilla bands may wear down Portuguese resistance.

Economically, northern Angola is important to the country's economy. Coffee is the principal cash crop in this region. Forty-eight per cent of the export value is in coffee. Interestingly, coffee trees on plantations owned by Portuguese have not been totally destroyed by Africans. Both sides hope to harvest the 1961 coffee crop.

Politically, the situation in the north has alerted Africans in central and southern Angola to the existing conflict between the Portuguese government and Africans. Government raids and arrests of educated Africans throughout Angola have created a bond among the villagers of all ethnic groups. The "bush telegraph" carries news from the north to the remotest corner in Angola, emphasizing the successes achieved by Angolan Africans against the Portuguese. Government officials are asking: "Will the Cuanhamas, the Ovimbundu, the Lundas, follow in the footsteps of the Kikongos and Kimbundu-speaking groups?" The Portuguese are already in serious trouble in Portuguese Congo. If other tribes join in the rebellion, the Portuguese government will be in a desperate situation. She will have to commit all her military forces to defend Angola. There is doubt whether Portugal can subdue a united African revolt of four and a half million people.

The role of the Congo government is also of great importance. Military supplies for Angolan nationalists must come by way of the Congo border. A friendly Congolese government will facilitate the carrying on of a prolonged guerrilla war. Training camps could be established across the border. Sixty thousand Angolan refugees are reported to have fled to the Congo. Many of these are eager to receive training in guerrilla tactics, hoping to gain revenge against the Portuguese for the killings and the destruction of their villages. The prospect of a stable Congo government would immensely help Angolan Africans in their battle against the Portuguese. The 480 miles of Congo border is ideal terrain through which to slip arms, men and supplies into Angola. The Portuguese cannot guard every inch of their northern border. This move would not only involve Africans of the Bakongo tribe, but other Angolans living in the Katanga and Kasai provinces. The problem is one of coordination.

## Portuguese Tactics of Division and Retaliation

The Portuguese government realizes that in order to hold on to Angola, it must divide the Africans. There are many ways to accomplish this. The most obvious method is to use troops recruited from the south to fight the rebels from the north. Nova Lisboa and Silva Porto in central Angola are the training centers for these African contingents. In addition to army recruits from the south, the government has intensified its contract labor program in order to supply workers for the coffee region. An expedient measure employed in recruiting labor for the coffee-picking task is to sentence political prisoners to work in that area.

Tribal divisions are intensified as the press plays up the loyalty of the Bailundu workers during attacks by African rebels. An article appearing in the newspaper, *O Lobito*, during late 1961 illustrates this publicity campaign. Bearing the heading, "A Good And Loyal Dedication Of A Bailundu Who Fought Side By Side With His Employer Whose Death He Deplores Deeply," the interview begins with these words:

Before us is a Bailundu, Pedro José, who has been wounded in both arms while in the north of Angola. It is of interest to hear of his loyalty and to hear also of other loyal Angolans, of whom there are many in this Portuguese province. At this moment our thoughts are with those who

were massacred while defending our country where peace always reigned
between blacks and whites without conflict. For the first time I present
to the press of our country one of these humble and brave Portuguese of
the black race. We know how he feels. We sympathize with him in his
loss of his employer.

Weekly accounts of similar stories of bravery by loyal Bailundus
appear in the press. In June the manager of the Gonçalves and
Tristão *fazenda* proposed that the loyal Bailundus be armed. He
stated that by arming the Bailundus, they could defend themselves
from these attacks and would be able to hunt for the "terrorists" in
the forests. "This," he said, "is one of the best ways to fight the
enemy." Military men who participated in the early campaigns of
occupation and pacification in Angola also concur.

Another tactic is the government's order to village leaders to report any stranger found within their midst. Often this has meant a
specific directive to an African group, such as the Chissanji-speak-
ing people of the coastal area, to turn over to the government post
any Ovimbundu passing through their villages. Extension of the
order would result in the Ganguelas reporting on the Ovimbundu,
or the Ovimbundu turning in a Chokwe, or a Kimbundu capturing
a Kikongo. This is a deliberate policy of the Portuguese government.
They justify their actions by stating that enmity between African
groups is inherent within their tribal culture.

Another method used by the Portuguese to breed dissension
among the peoples of Angola is the use of radio broadcasts. One station is located in the city of Silva Porto in central Angola. The hour
of the broadcast is 1:10 P.M. on the 41-meter band. Two Africans,
Artur Sapasa and Rebecca Lufita—both enrolled in the school of
nursing at the government hospital—broadcast the news of the day
in their own language, Umbundu. Their message is, first, hate the
Americans and, second, fight the terrorists in the north. The campaign to hate Americans is based on racial discrimination in the
United States. They claim that U.S. Negroes are slaves to the white
man. "Be careful," the announcers warn, "of Americans in your
midst. Their aim is to make you slaves as they have done to the
Negroes in the United States."

Enmity towards the people of the north is fostered by describing the massacre of women and children and the killing of loyal Bailundus by the terrorists. "We are Portuguese," they announce, "and we must defend ourselves from these invaders who come from outside. Do you want to be like the Congo, where women and children are hungry? This is stupidity on our part to think that we can live independently of the Portuguese." Informed Africans say, when questioned about the effect of these broadcasts: "We listen to them, but we know that Artur and Rebecca are forced by the Portuguese to make the broadcasts." However, the repeated attacks on Americans and on the terrorists are sowing seeds of dissension. A continued Portuguese policy of this nature makes real the possibility of another chaotic Congo in Angola.

Religion is also being used by the Portuguese to divide the peoples of Angola. Protestant-Catholic relations have been strained because of the accusation leveled by the government against Protestants as being one of the responsible organizations for terrorist activities in northern Angola. Two newspapers, *Província de Angola,* a Luanda daily, and *O Planalto,* a bi-weekly publication in Nova Lisboa, have led the anti-Protestant campaign. The repeated accusations by civilians and officials have resulted in the arrest of many Protestant leaders. Baptist and Methodist groups have suffered most. Of the sixty-five ordained ministers in the Methodist Conference, thirteen are in prison, five are dead, eleven are missing and thirty-six are refugees or are still in service. The Luanda district reveals the severity of the government attacks: of the one hundred sixty-five ministers, pastors and teachers under the care of the Conference, twenty-eight are in prison, seven are dead, ninety are unaccounted for, and thirty are still in service.

In central Angola, Protestants have also been persecuted by the Portuguese populace. The Bocoio and Balombo areas were targets of the campaigns against Protestants. In Bocoio during Easter week, the Protestant pastor and church elders were arrested and beaten by the police. They were accused by the *chefe de posto* of being leaders of a terrorist plot. What was the evidence? European shopkeepers reported an unusual demand for salt in their district. They surmised that Bocoio people were making salt bombs; but the real reason for the hoarding of salt was simply that the Africans were afraid that a shortage of salt was imminent because of the unsettled conditions. The prisoners were sent to Lobito for interrogation by PIDE.

At the village level, government persecutions intensified the rivalry between Catholics and Protestants. Catholic villages have been relatively free from government raids—a situation that has not gone unquestioned by the Protestants. The attitude of some Catholic converts has also contributed to the strained relationship between these two groups. In the Ganguela area to the south, Protestants accuse Catholics of dressing themselves up as *Oviganji* (evil spirits) for the purpose of scaring Protestant groups during church services. Intense feelings of animosity are created by constant friction at the village level.

Arrests and killings of Protestant church leaders not only heighten the division within the Portuguese province, but also affect existing political groups working for an independent Angola. The Leopoldville group (União de Populações de Angola) has been said to favor Protestants, while the Conakry group (Movimento Popular de Libertação de Angola) represents Catholics. The persecution of Protestants within Angola by Portuguese authorities has sharpened the existing division between the Leopoldville and Conakry groups.

These Portuguese tactics designed to divide the Africans are supplemented by tactics of direct and repressive retaliatory measures against African revolt and violence. Portuguese troops, of which twenty-five to thirty thousand were already stationed in Angola by the end of June 1961, have been vicious in their retaliatory measures. Thirteen different kinds of brutalities against Africans were attributed to the Portuguese troops in a document published on June 18, 1961 (and quoted in the Manchester *Guardian* four days later) by the members of the British Baptist Missionary Society stationed in the Portuguese Congo. These missionaries accused the Portuguese military authorities of making reprisals against rebellious Africans with the "utmost barbarism, lynching and slaughtering tens of thousands of men, women and children."

The police, too, have participated in the campaign to crush the Angolan revolt. In Luanda hundreds of Africans were arrested by PIDE during April 1961. The cities of central Angola—Lobito, Benguela, Nova Lisboa and Silva Porto—were combed for the reported terrorists in their midst. *Assimilados* were especially in danger of arrest, for a terrorist was described as a well-dressed person possessing a *bilhete de identidade* and wearing dark glasses. The Portuguese referred to them as *calçinhos* (one who wears European trousers). Police raided student dormitories, searched students' belongings, made wholesale arrests, and even resorted to beatings in order to extract evidence. One tragic case involved a student studying at the *liceu* in Nova Lisboa. On hearing that PIDE wished to see him, the student innocently presented himself to the police. "After all," he remarked, "I have nothing to hide." The student was last seen by his friends at five o'clock that afternoon. One month later, the "grapevine" reported that he had died in prison in Lobito. Friends speculate that he died as a result of injuries sustained during repeated beatings by PIDE in Nova Lisboa and Lobito.

The police will continue to play an important role in the suppression of African nationalism. Since the wave of arrests that erupted in April 1960, the corps of security police has added six hundred guards to its ranks and has opened branches in all the major cities.

Police and civilian retaliatory measures show that the Portuguese reacted from fear. PIDE continuously uncovered plots against the state, and the pattern of these plots assumed a monotonous similarity: the revolt was always discovered twenty-four or forty-eight hours before it was scheduled to break out; during these raids PIDE uncovered lists with names of Europeans who were to be liquidated; inevitably, letters were found linking the rebels with outside forces, especially with those of the late Patrice Lumumba. PIDE's favorite hour of arrest was midnight or during the early morning hours.

A typical plot was that of Sá da Bandeira. On June 10, 1961, which is a Portuguese national holiday, all African gasoline pump attendants in the city were ordered by their leaders to spray the streets with gasoline fifteen minutes before the start of the day's festive parade. When the parade began, the attendants were to light a match to the gasoline. The governor of the district, merchants, soldiers, would be burned to death and the plotters could then seize the city. Needless to say, the plot did not materialize. Three plots were discovered in Nova Lisboa, two at Novo Redondo, and one at

Port Alexandre. The latter plan supposedly awaited help from Russian fishing ships plying along the Angolan coast. The leaders were arrested by PIDE forty-eight hours before the expected revolt.

Police and army retaliatory measures have been greatly influenced by the *colonos*. Africans report that 1,500 people in the Luanda district were killed by white civilians in May when Europeans raided African homes located in the African section of the city. Men were yanked from their homes by white vigilantes and shot without trial. Civilian actions were extreme. In some cases responsible authorities protested, but this did not stop the Europeans' campaign to liquidate all educated Africans. In the coffee region of the Calulu administration, for example, the government doctor protested the brutal measures taken against Africans by white civilians. His protests were brushed aside and the civilian population threatened to kill him for obstructing their actions. At that, the doctor hastily gathered his belongings and fled. No one dared to protest the retaliatory measures by civilians no matter how flagrant. In Luanda, for instance, any white Portuguese refugee from the disturbed Congo could accuse an African of being one of the rebels. "Look, look," he would shout, pointing to an African, "he's one of the *terroristas*." Without hesitation armed civilians would shoot and kill the defenseless African. Police did not interfere with the actions of civilians. The creation of the *Corpos de Voluntários* (C.P.) on March 31, 1961, by order of the President of the Council and the Overseas Minister, cloaked civilian actions with respectability and legality. This Voluntary Corps is an auxiliary organization of the armed forces. They cooperate with the military in the internal security of the province and in its defense against the outside enemy. Eventually the Voluntary Corps is to be the civil defense organization of the territory. Civilian retaliatory actions reflect Lisbon Political and Social Studies Center Professor George Dias' analysis of the Portuguese character. Professor Dias writes in the Center's publication, *The Expansion of the Portuguese Overseas* ("Inquiry on Anti-Colonialism"): "The Portuguese man is, above all, profoundly humane and kindhearted, without being weak. He does not like to make others suffer and he avoids conflict, but when ill-treated and hurt in his pride he may become violent and even cruel."

## African Reaction to Portuguese Tactics

During the months from March through June of 1961, the Africans were left helpless, exposed to attacks by white civilians. Portuguese legalization of white civilian actions against Africans often meant the total collapse of judicial procedures in some parts of Angola. Every educated African became a suspect, punishable by the civilian population. Any African could accuse another of a political crime, with resultant arrest by the security police.

Africans reacted differently to this situation in different parts of Angola. In the Portuguese Congo, people fled across the border into the Republic of the Congo, especially when Portuguese troops began to bomb and strafe villages. Over 100,000 refugees had crossed into the Congo Republic up to the end of July 1961. Mrs. David Grenfell, a British Baptist missionary who worked twenty-one years in the Portuguese Congo, said in an interview published in the Manchester *Guardian* (June 29, 1961), that in their area Africans were not afraid of the rebels. There was no doubt in her mind that the action of the police in dropping incendiary bombs on villages and in taking away the male population caused Africans to flee. "Many men," she continued, "have simply disappeared."

While the people from Portuguese Congo fled across the border, Africans in Luanda and central Angola were in a much more difficult position. Escape via the sea was impossible owing to the lack of transportation. The borders of Republic of the Congo, the Rhodesias and South-West Africa were too far away. Patrolling of the frontiers by the police further complicated any movement towards these borders.

In such a situation, reactions of Africans differed widely. Those living in the north were more militant in their attitude towards the Portuguese: they had nothing to lose, for their villages were already destroyed. This was the attitude also of Africans in the Luanda district. Hundreds of educated Africans were in prison, and they hoped the world would hear of their plight. They were ready to face the inevitable retaliatory measures when Portuguese authorities discovered the sources of information.

Africans in central Angola, however, were cautious in their reactions. When the revolt began in the north, they adopted a "let's wait and see" attitude, not realizing that they would be involved in the struggle taking place in the Portuguese Congo. After the first attacks, security police arrested over two hundred educated Africans. Soon Africans in central Angola began to say, "The war in the north is only causing us trouble. This is the fault of the United Nations. Why did they encourage this rebellion if they can't help us?" A sixty-year-old African, commenting on the troubled times, remarked, "I often wish for the good old days when all we had to do was to pay our taxes and work on the road." This attitude is understandable as Africans in central Angola have no way of escape; they are at the mercy of the police and government officials. Hence, many of the educated Africans scattered to their villages, integrating their lives into the existing communal pattern. As long as their villages are safe from incendiary bombs, they will remain there with their families. But their safety is precarious, for the police network extends into the villages where Africans are recruited as informers by PIDE.

Ironically, African students in primary and secondary educational programs benefited from the confusion caused by the war. All were given a bonus of two and one-half points on their final examination papers. For instance, a student receiving a grade of six in his written exams added the extra points to make a total of eight and one-half, which admits him to the orals. This generous gesture by the government produced fantastic results. In Benguela one hundred fifty students took their first cycle examinations covering the first two years of high school. Of this number, only two failed. Furthermore, of the one hundred forty-eight who passed the written tests, two-thirds were excused from taking the orals. The results of the primary grades were also comparable. In one of the rural schools only four failed out of eighty students presented. Ordinarily this school had less than 50 per cent of their students passing. Angolan students in Portugal reacted differently. A total of forty-one fled from their studies in Lisbon and Coimbra during the months of May and June. Three students feared that they would be recalled for military service. The other left because they suspected that PIDE planned to arrest them for security reasons. All forty-one are enrolled in universities in England, France, Switzerland, Germany and the United States.

## Voice of the Church

The war in northern Angola has also involved the world religious community. Portuguese officials blame Protestant missions for the terrorism in the north. They reason that foreign missionaries are responsible for denationalizing the Africans, resulting in an African revolt against the ruling authorities. The Portuguese also point out that no Protestant missionaries and their families were attacked by African nationalists despite the fact that many of their Portuguese neighbors were killed. Luanda newspapers charged that Protestant missions distributed seditious pamphlets prior to the attacks in the north.

When Portuguese refugees from the north were evacuated to Luanda, white groups joined with them to attack the Methodist mission property in that city. The public health clinic located in the Museque, the African section, was destroyed by the attackers. They also set fire to the school building. But a greater loss to the Methodist work was the killing of eight African pastors, either shot down by armed white civilians or executed by soldiers after hurried trials.

A Baptist missionary, the Rev. Clifford J. Parsons, confirmed the report of the Methodists. At a session of the Baptist Union of Britain and Ireland on May 1, Mr. Parsons declared that thousands of Africans have been slaughtered and mutilated. He stated that he had never experienced such a spirit of hatred as is in existence now in Angola. In his address, Mr. Parsons quoted a Portuguese doctor: "They started it. They had no mercy on our women and children. They will pay for this in full." Mr. Parsons further asserted that the outbreaks of violence were prompted by a combination of the growing strength of African nationalism, and that the African's patience has finally run out.[7]

In offering a resolution deploring the state of affairs in Angola, Mr. Parsons commended the Roman Catholic hierarchy for their recent pastoral letter. Four bishops and one archbishop denounced terrorism, but called for a redress of grievances. They said: "Disillusioned people fighting against privation are a prey to despair and more apt to be carried away by dangerous ideologies and promises which cannot be fulfilled. Poverty is a bad counselor and is a threat to tranquillity and peace. The solution of certain problems can be found only through united and adequate legislation and the total and generous cooperation of individuals and organizations. The Church is entirely within the limits of its mission in advising citizens to unite themselves for the moralization of laws and institutions, and for the formation of a more perfect social situation, supported by justice and charity."

There is grave doubt, however, whether it will be possible at this time to formulate "a more perfect social situation, supported by justice and charity." The situation in Angola has reached a "point of no return." Extermination is the policy of both the whites and the blacks. The voices of the moderates are no longer heard. Events have moved too fast; the voice for a more perfect social situation has come too late.

## The Myth of a Multiracial Society

World opinion has been shocked by the intense hatred displayed by both sides. Portuguese cite the killing of a Capuchin monk in the town of Damba as an example of African savagery. When African nationalists approached the town, thirty-three-year-old Father Pedro Juan from Trieste walked towards the attackers, holding a crucifix above his head. He urged them to stop, but the Africans continued advancing. They shot him down, heedless of the priest's prayers.[8] Africans, on the other hand, point to the village of Soya as an illustration of Portugal's policy of extermination. One old woman told a reporter her family had been almost completely wiped out by Portuguese troops. She and her husband had managed to escape with her daughter's two little babies.[9]

Where is the racial harmony in Angola of which the Portuguese boasted? It was a myth. Angolan Africans do not love their rulers. They say:

> We no longer wish to have some other arrangement with the Portuguese or even to talk about some other arrangement with them. All that we care for is to have our own land. We do not wish anything else from the Portuguese. We do not wish to have the country of Portugal joined to ours any longer. From the beginning this country in which we are has been ours. Of olden times it was a separate land and the people thereof a different people. Long ago it was seized by those who were sent here for that purpose. Their race is a different one, their speech and their habits are different. We do not wish to have them lie to us, saying: "You and we are both Portuguese." It is not true. They say it only with their mouths. In their hearts, it is not there. In their hearts there is race prejudice. If this were not the case how would things be as they are?
>
> All opportunities for employment go to the Portuguese. We Africans do not get a chance to work. Every place that could be filled by an educated person has become theirs. We see no way of supporting our families or ourselves. Everything is theirs while we and our children are left to die of hunger.
>
> They of Portugal are what they are: they have nothing in common with us, even as we have nothing in common with them. For from the beginning of the world until today Angola was a different place and likewise Portugal was another place. All that we wish is to let things be as God arranged them. We only wish to keep the relationship of our blood—that is all. . . . We state the matter thus: Let them keep to their own blood and we for our part shall belong to our blood. Let their blood be dominant in their country while ours in our country will be dominant here.[10]

The March violence in northern Angola demonstrates the depth of this feeling. Portugal ignores this fact, continuing to claim Angola as Portuguese. There is doubt whether Portugal can hold onto her position in Angola beyond 1962.

### The Effects upon Angola of Violence and Crisis

War in Angola has greatly changed this Portuguese province. In an administrative shuffle, Salazar recalled Dr. Silva Tavares and named General Venâncio Deslandes, former Ambassador to Spain, as the new governor-general of Angola. The significance of this replacement lies in the return to a military official as the head of the Angolan government. Dr. Silva Tavares, had been the second civilian to occupy this post since the beginning of the Portuguese occupation five hundred years ago. General Deslandes was instructed to merge the civilian and military functions of the government during this emergency period. The priority of military functions was indicated by General Deslandes in his speech upon his commissioning in Lisbon, in June 1961, as the new governor-general of Angola: "They (the nationalists) have made war upon us. There are now only two roads—unconditional surrender or extermination." To carry out the policy of military primacy and the extermination of the nationalists, General Deslandes appointed four military men as district governors in the north of Angola, the area of greatest revolt and violence.

An important social change was brought about in Angola by the revolt in the Portuguese Congo, which shattered the Portuguese myth of the existence of a multiracial society in Angola. The conflict there is a racial war. Portuguese authorities blame UPA for creating the present chasm between blacks and whites. Africans, however, deny this accusation of the UPA. They say, "The only place where racism did not exist was in bed." In his "Inquiry on Anti-Colonialism," in the Lisbon Political and Social Studies Center's publication titled *The Expansion of the Portuguese Overseas*, Professor George Dias substantiates this observation: "The Portuguese, led by healthy instinct, mixed with the various populations of the world, contributing highly to racial fusion. It was the free exercise of this impulse that led him to consider men as his equals and made him love women of all colors." But all too often the Portuguese "love of women of all colors" did not extend beyond the "healthy instinct." The Portuguese version of the creation myth reflects the Portuguese racial prejudice in other areas of behavior. According to the *chefe de posto* of the Sambo district, the explanation for the whiteness of the palms of Africans' hands is this:

When God created the white man, the Devil became jealous and decided to create his own man. When the devil saw that what he had created was black, he dowsed him in the river. He scrubbed and scrubbed him, but the black creature remained black. In exasperation, the devil punched him on the nose. As the black man fell, he put out his hands to break his fall and the palms of his hands pressed into the white clay. This is the explanation of why the black man's nose is flat and why the palms of his hands are white.

The principal economic effect of the war in Angola has been a financial crisis. The announcement by the government of an emergency loan of 5,000,000 escudos, or $17,500,000, from the Bank of Angola to carry on such necessary military projects as construction of airfields, roads, communication lines, is a sign of the pressing financial burden of the war. Further loans from the Bank of Angola is inevitable, although the government's proposal to increase taxes on gasoline and luxury goods in Portugal may help considerably in underwriting the cost of the war. Specifically, the government decree levied taxes (1) on tobacco manufactured in Portugal and foreign countries; (2) on every bottle of beer and other cold drinks of approximately 1¾ cents; (3) an increase in the automobile tax within the country; (4) a further charge of 3½ cents on each liter of gasoline; (5) an increase in income, land, loan and construction taxes. In his announcement, the Finance Minister stressed the temporary character of these measures. Many Portuguese, on the other hand, doubt that these increases are of a temporary nature. The revolt in Angola has taken on the aspect of another Algerian war.

Furthermore, the prospect of the loss of the coffee crop in the Portuguese Congo is discouraging to the European settlers in Angola. Harvesting begins in June and continues through July and August, ending just before the onset of the rainy season. The 1961 coffee yield would not have affected the Angolan economy had it not been harvested, as 1960's production was withheld from the world coffee market, but the psychological effect upon the settlers would have been disastrous. According to Portuguese sources, two-thirds of the 1961 crop was harvested. The government hopes that the European settlers will interpret this as meaning that Angola is not lost as a Portuguese province and that those who have left Angola will return.

Government regulations have also stopped the flight of capital from Angola. Angolan residents are forbidden to transfer money to Lisbon without permission from bank authorities, and this is granted for only limited sums. As a result, requests for dollar checks by Portuguese residents plague foreign organizations and residents. The demand increased the value of the U.S. dollar from escudos 29$60 to 32$50.

The personal life of the Portuguese resident in Angola is also affected by the war situation. Men between the ages of seventeen and forty-five are discouraged from leaving the country. Those who attempt to leave are called traitors. If permission is granted to leave Angola, the male resident must purchase a round-trip ticket. Otherwise, officials could make it difficult for him to obtain the necessary exit documents.

Not only is the male resident restricted in his movements to leave the country, but he is obligated to do sentry duty. Every European village has its vigilance committee which directs security measures of the white population. Arms are issued indiscriminately to all European men who request them. Often the knowledge by Africans that the Portuguese possessed guns prejudiced trade in the European towns. African males remained in their villages and sent the women out to buy such minimum necessary household items as sugar, fish and corn meal. Formerly, villages on Saturday mornings were crowded with buyers from the countryside. But during the months of April, May, and June 1961, Saturday mornings were like any other business day of the week. A trader in Bela Vista stated that prior to the disturbances, he averaged a gross trade volume of seven contos (approximately $245) daily; in June he averaged one conto, or $35. The overt patriotic activities of the traders prejudiced the commercial activities in all Portuguese towns.

Portugal, however, is determined to hold onto Angola as an overseas province. Civilian groups and government authorities have rallied around Salazar. Angolans are forbidden to refer to themselves as *"Nós Angolanos"* (We Angolans). They must say *"Nós Portuguesas"* (We Portuguese). Any newspaper reference to an event as being for the "good of Angola" must be changed to a *"bem da nação Portuguesa"*—good for the Portuguese nation. But there is European opposition in Angola to the colonial policy of the Salazar regime. In the month of June, for example, three men—one in Lobito and two in Benguela—were arrested for plotting against the security of the state. The three—a civil engineer, a *liceu* teacher and a commercial trader—circulated a petition requesting the Lisbon authorities to grant Angola an autonomous government. All were apprehended and sent to the Luanda prison. Opposition to Salazar is equivalent to detention by PIDE. Nevertheless, political anecdotes ridiculing the dictatorial Salazar regime are frequently heard in Angolan European circles.

One such anecdote relates how President Américo Tomás, Premier Salazar and the Overseas Minister decided to board a plane in Lisbon for an aerial view of the many improvements made by the government during the past twenty years. As the plane circled over Lisbon, Premier Salazar turned to his colleagues and declared, "I'm so happy this morning, I must share my happiness with my countrymen." He took a one hundred escudo note from his billfold and threw it overboard, saying, "This will make one other Portuguese happy." Thereupon, President Américo Tomás took out a five hundred escudo note from his billfold, tossed it out, and said, "This will make five Portuguese happy." The Overseas Minister, not to be outdone by his President and Premier, fished out a thousand escudo note from his wallet, threw it overboard, and said, "This will make ten Portuguese happy." Then the three passengers heard the pilot chuckling to himself. "Come," said Salazar to the pilot, "you must tell us why you are laughing." "Oh, no, I can't," replied the pilot, "my thoughts are my own." "Don't be afraid," prompted Salazar, "no one will harm you." "All right," answered the pilot. "I know how to make eight million Portuguese happy." "But how is that possible?" inquired Salazar. "Eight million Portuguese would be happy," declared the pilot, "if I threw all three of you overboard."

To counteract the influence of the opposition, the government sponsored patriotic rallies, especially in the cities and towns situated along the Benguela railway. Africans are urged to appear at these functions and to listen to speeches by government representatives. A well-known apologist of the government is a *mestiço*, António de Almeida Alves, a photographer turned orator. Senhor Alves speaks the African language, Umbundu, fluently, but it is difficult to measure the extent of Senhor Alves' influence among his African audiences.

## The Effect upon International Opinion of Violence in Angola

The violence in northern Angola has not escaped the attention of the world. In London the formation of a Council for Freedom in Portugal and Colonies was announced on March 29, 1961. Three Labor members of Parliament and fifty prominent Britons are sponsors. The aims of the Council are: "To bring together friends in Britain of freedom in Portugal and her colonies; to work with those in Portugal and in her colonies who are struggling for freedom, independence, and human rights; to operate through all parties in Parliament and on public opinion to influence British government policy in support of these objectives in the United Nations; through the North Atlantic Treaty Organization and other international organizations." [5]

The vice-chairmen, Sir Leslie Monroe and Viscount Stansgate, declared that the immediate objective of the group is to persuade the British government to take a firmer stand against the Portuguese policy in its colonies. Sir Leslie pointed out that Britain has abstained in votes on United Nations resolutions to inquire into the situation in Portuguese Angola. "We want," he said, "to put pressure on our government to support such an inquiry."

The direction of world opinion, however, focussed on the fifteenth session of the United Nations General Assembly. The situation in Angola was listed as agenda item 92 and the resolution read as follows:

The General Assembly, taking note of the recent disturbances and conflicts in Angola resulting in loss of life of the inhabitants, the continuance of which is likely to endanger the maintenance of international peace and security,

Viewing with concern the growing restiveness of dependent peoples throughout the world for self-determination and independence,

Aware that failure to act speedily, effectively and in time for ameliorating the disabilities of the African peoples of Angola is likely to endanger international peace and security,

Recalling General Assembly resolution 1514 (XV) of 14 December 1960, by which the General Assembly declared without dissent that the subjection of peoples to alien subjugation, domination and exploitation constitutes a denial of fundamental human rights, is contrary to the Charter of the United Nations and is an impediment to the promotion of world peace and co-operation and asked for immediate steps to be taken to transfer all powers to the peoples of those territories, without any conditions or reservations, in accordance with their freely expressed will and desire, without any distinction as to race, creed or colour, in order to enable them to enjoy complete independence and freedom,

Recalling further General Assembly resolutions 1541 (XV) and 1542 (XV) of 15 December 1960,

1. Calls upon the Government of Portugal to consider urgently the introduction of measures and reforms in Angola for the purpose of the implementation of General Assembly resolution 1514 (XV) of 14 December 1960, with due respect for human rights and fundamental freedoms and in accordance with the Charter;

2. Decides to appoint a sub-committee consisting of five and instructs this sub-committee to examine the statements made before the General Assembly concerning Angola, to receive further statements and documents and to conduct such inquiries as it may deem necessary and to report to the General Assembly as soon as possible.

The General Assembly adopted the resolution on April 20 by a vote of 73 to 2. Spain and the Union of South Africa registered the negative votes. The resolution was sponsored by all member African nations; but most of them were skeptical about what an investigative committee could do in the absence of Portuguese cooperation. Furthermore, when the Angolan resolution was being considered, the Cuban invasion and the participation of the United States in it were the critical issues on the agenda. The acceptance of the Angolan resolution by the General Assembly hardly created a by-line in the newspapers.

Two and a half weeks after the adjournment of the Assembly, the chief Soviet delegate to the United Nations, Valerian A. Zorin, complained to Frederick H. Boland of Ireland, president of the fifteenth session, that the United Nations had not taken the necessary urgent steps to halt Portuguese oppression in Angola. Mr. Boland's office denied that there was any deliberate attempt to forestall action on the General Assembly's resolution. Mr. Boland's spokesman said that five nations had already been invited to join the investigative sub-committee and he expected to have their replies shortly. This action of the General Assembly raised the hopes of some Africans in Angola. Implementation of the resolution, however, is remote. Consequently, the General Assembly's resolution was a gesture of concern by member nations over the situation in Angola, rather than a workable policy to halt Portuguese oppression in her West African territory.

Another international organization involved is the North Atlantic Treaty Organization. At the ministers' conference of that body held in Norway on May 8, 1961, NATO's structure was threatened by Portugal's anger at her allies who had voted in favor of the Angolan resolution. Portugal's Foreign Minister, Alberto Franco Nogueira, privately denounced her allies, especially the United States, for criticizing her policy in Angola. Furthermore, Portugal will not hesitate to use in Angola her troops earmarked for NATO's defense. The Portuguese point to France's use of her NATO troops in fighting the war in Algeria. The reply by the Norwegian Foreign Minister, Halvard Lange, to the Council of Ministers isolated the Portuguese further from her NATO partners. He said that while Norway sympathizes with Portugal, she could not close her eyes to the elemental force of nationalism in Africa and felt obliged to vote accordingly in the United Nations.[6] The only development that came from the Council of Ministers' meeting to appease Portuguese feelings was a plan to establish temporary committees for improving the confused state of political consultation within the alliance. These committees, consisting of the nations with a direct interest in a given area such as Asia or Africa, would attempt to keep members aligned on or aware of policy differences in matters where alliance partners might become involved in embarrassing conflicts.

Reports have not indicated Portuguese reactions to the differences in policy matters she encountered at the ministers' council. For African nationalists in Angola, the threat by Portugal to use her NATO forces is serious. These forces are well equipped and are trained under NATO's command. Such a move may force Portugal to resign from the North Atlantic Treaty Organization. Portugal would then be free to act without the irritation of being criticized by members of a group of which she is a member. In Europe, such a step will force Portugal to ally herself with Spain in an Iberian defense pact. In Africa, Portugal will make overtures to the South African government for closer military and political cooperation. The Portuguese ideal of the multiracial society would be replaced by a policy of extreme white supremacy.

# 7. WHAT OF THE FUTURE?

The future status of Angola is tied to the Congo, economically and politically. For Katanga, the Angolan Benguela railway is important. It is the shortest and easiest transport outlet for her mineral ores. What are the alternate routes if the Benguela railway is closed? First, there is the all-Congo rail and river route from Elizabethville to Leopoldville and Matadi, either via Port Francqui and the Kasai River (1,720 miles with two transshipments) or via Bukama, Kabalo and Stanleyville (2,235 miles with seven transshipments); next, there is the Congo-Tanganyika route by river, lake and rail to Dar-es-Salaam (1,717 miles with four transshipments); then there is the 1,619-mile Rhodesia-Mozambique all-rail route to Beira; and finally, there is the Rhodesia–Union of South Africa rail route to Capetown or other South African ports (2,300 miles).[1]

The advantages of the Lobito route via the Benguela railway are obvious: shipment from Elizabethville to Lobito takes only eight days; from Elizabethville to Matadi via the Congo River route takes twenty-four days, with two transshipments while the Elizabethville-Beira route takes twelve days, with a longer ocean route from the latter port to Angola's European and American markets. The importance of the Benguela railway to the economic development of the Katanga region in the Congo is evident. The Leopoldville group could easily enlist the sympathy and aid of the leaders of Katanga for a united action against the Portuguese.

The recent and repeated political schisms in the Congo make the likelihood of "balkanization" in Angola real. The Abako leaders in Angola know that a confederation of states operates on the principle that the bigger and wealthier the state, the stronger bargaining power it possesses, as evidenced by the role Tshombe played in the negotiations at the conference at Tananarive in Malagasy, and even in later Congo politics. The way for Abako to increase its number and wealth is to invite the Kikongo-speaking people of the Portuguese Congo to join its party. Such action can split Angola into small units. Each tribe may establish its own state: the Kimbundus in Luanda, the Ovimbundu in Huambo and the Cuanyamas in Cuamato. The future of a "balkanized" Angola would be dim. The 4,500,000 people within an area of 480,000 square miles must act as a unit if they hope to survive.

Angola's future is not only contingent upon the situation in the Congo, but will also depend upon *how* independence in Angola is attained. Many factors are involved. If the Portuguese use tribal divisions to forestall the African demand for independence (for example, using Ovimbundu soldiers to put down riots among the Kikongos), the Congo nightmare can be reenacted. An example is the killing of whites living in the Portuguese Congo by Africans on March 17, 1961. Portuguese authorities declare that large numbers of Bailundu tribesmen (Ovimbundu), who have been working as contract laborers in the coffee plantations, fought off the Bakongo tribesmen and cooperated closely with the Portuguese. Dormant tribal rivalries can be reawakened in Angola.[2]

A second factor is that if disagreements among the nationalist movements develop into open divisions (for example, UPA *vs.* FRAIN), there is danger of an ideological conflict. The association of UPA with the Kasavubu group raises many doubts among the leaders of FRAIN. The Conakry group is suspicious of Kasavubu for two reasons: the implication of his government in the assassination of Patrice Lumumba, and Kasavubu's stand in favor of regionalism as opposed to a centralized government. The Congo disaster can be duplicated unless UPA and FRAIN settle their differences. Only a single political party can mold Angola into one nation.

Third, if the Portuguese continue to refuse to give independence to Angola, the outcome will be increased violence. The reported killing of whites by Africans on March 17, 1961, was the beginning of such terrorism. The *New York Times* reported forty to one hundred persons killed and wounded.[3] Increasing violence will cause enormous loss of life and property. The need for rehabilitation of industry and government would increase a hundredfold. Yet many Africans will pursue this course of desperation if there is no other

way. Leaders of African nationalist groups will lose control of their
followers. Chaos will result.

Lastly, the question—Is Angola ready for independence?—also
depends upon how independence is attained. The Portuguese claim
that disaster will be the consequence if Angola is given her independence in 1962. They cite these facts: in Angola there are only
two African doctors, no engineers, no lawyers, no agronomists. How
can the Africans, the Portuguese ask, govern Angola without uni-
versity-trained personnel? The Portuguese point to events in the
Congo as a prime example of why they should not give Angola her
independence.

Angolan Africans are aware of the lack of trained professional
and civil service personnel. But they reply: Who is to blame for
this situation? Is it not the fault of the Portuguese? We were ready
twenty years ago for higher education, but the unfair selective system of Portuguese education hindered our progress. Africans state
that independence does not mean expulsion of all Portuguese from
Angola. They invite Europeans to remain and work with them for
a prosperous and democratic Angola. The basis for cooperation,
however, must be equality. Another alternative is to ask the United
Nations and other African countries for technical assistance. Other
Africans say the question is not whether Angola is ready for independence, but how they can help Angola become an independent
nation.

It is important to emphasize again that the clash in Angola is
between the two nationalisms: Portuguese on one hand, African on
the other. Dr. Vasco Vierra Garin, Portugal's representative to the
United Nations, speaks for Portuguese nationalism when he declares:

The fact remains that my country does not practice any type whatever of colonialism within the Portuguese nation. Portugal has been for
centuries a unitary nation, and it has always been recognized as such
by the international community. We are a multiracial nation, as many
other nations; our land and our people are dispersed over several continents, as is also the case with other nations, but we comprise only one
unit, completely independent and solid—politically, juridically, and socially—one country with the same strong national feeling.[4]

FRAIN expresses African nationalism in these words:

The African anti-colonialist organizations of the Portuguese colonies, representing the legitimate aspirations of their people, want to reestablish the human dignity of Africans, their freedom, and the right to determine their own future. These organizations want the people to enjoy real social development based on fruitful work and economic progress, on African unity and fraternity. . . .[5]

The two views are irreconcilable. Violence is the inevitable result of the conflict between the two views. The Portuguese will fight to retain their overseas possessions. The organizations for an independent Angola have maintained that since Portugal intends to use violence to defend her interests, they will be ready to answer with violence.

It is unfortunate that the Portuguese refuse to accept the validity of the widely recognized truth, which is stated particularly well by Thomas Hodgkin: ". . . the period of European ascendancy in Africa is drawing to an end, and concentration upon the problem how to ensure that its end does not inflict avoidable suffering upon Africans, Asians, or Europeans, would seem to be the only rational basis of any colonial Power." [6] The tragedy in Portuguese policy is that there is no rational basis for reconciling European and African nationalisms.

What courses of action are open? Pressures on Portugal through the United Nations and bilaterally, together with economic sanctions. England and the United States are in good positions from which to exercise pressure. They could see to the curtailment of the use of NATO arms, the withdrawal of capital from industrial and commercial operations, and the refusal to purchase Portuguese products. There will be, of course, a political by-product outside Angola. These policies will undermine Portugal's economic and political stability at home, even though directed at her overseas provinces. To offset this, the United States should offer Portugal economic aid, comparable to the Marshall Plan extended after World War II. Portugal's soil is fertile. She has adequate mineral resources and abundant hydroelectric power. The loss of Angola will not mean a lower standard of living for the Portuguese people. It will mean an end to the heroic myth. A new regime in Portugal can reverse the present domestic trend, which makes the rich richer and the poor poorer. It would, indeed, mean a new deal for the Portuguese.

But what about the Portuguese accusation that the disturbances in Angola are Communist inspired? This accusation is not founded on facts. Angolan nationalists want freedom to choose their own form of government. If the Portuguese continue to pursue their policy of the white man's rule, however, African nationalists may be driven into the Communist camp. The only way to have a free Angola is to give her independence. We are certain Angola will become independent. A *New York Times* editorial captured this historical reality in these words: "Governments cannot stop clocks or turn them back. This is 1961, not 1861 or 1561. Portuguese policy has been based on the belief that African nationalism would stop at the border of Angola and Mozambique, or be stopped. King Canute had as much chance of stopping the tide from coming in." [7]

Independence, with or without Portuguese cooperation, is the only way peace can be restored in war-torn Angola.

# APPENDIX I. DOCUMENTS

## Decree No. 18:570, July 8, 1930, Portuguese Colonial Act, Chapter II [1]

ARTICLE 15: The State shall guarantee the protection and defense of the natives in the colonies, in accordance with the principles of humanity and sovereignty, the provisions of this Chapter and the international conventions at present in force or which may come into force. The colonial authorities shall prevent and penalize all abuses against the persons and possessions of natives in accordance with the law.

ARTICLE 16: The State shall establish public institutions and encourage the creation of private ones to support the rights of natives or render them assistance. The institutions in either case shall be Portuguese.

ARTICLE 17: The law shall guarantee to the natives, under the terms stated therein, ownership and possession of their lands and crops and this principle must be respected in all concessions granted by the State.

ARTICLE 18: The labour of natives in the service of the State or in that of administrative bodies shall be remunerated.

ARTICLE 19: The following shall be prohibited: (1) All regulations according to which the State undertakes to furnish native labourers to any enterprises working for their own economic development. (2) All regulations according to which the natives existing in any territorial circumscription may be compelled to furnish labour to the said enterprises under any pretext whatever.

ARTICLE 20: The State may only compel natives to labour on public works of general benefit to the community, in occupations the results of which will be enjoyed by them, in execution of judicial decisions of a penal character or for the fulfilment of fiscal obligations.

ARTICLE 21: Regulations relating to the contracting of native labour shall be based on the liberty of the individual and on the right to a fair wage and assistance, the public authorities intervening only for purposes of supervision.

ARTICLE 22: Attention shall be paid in the colonies to the stage of evolution of the native populations, and there shall be special statutes for natives, which, under the authority of Portuguese public and private law, shall lay down juridical regulations for them in keeping with their individual, domestic and social usages and customs, provided that these are not incompatible with morality and dictates of humanity.

ARTICLE 23: The State shall ensure to all its overseas territories liberty of conscience and the free exercise of the various religions, subject to the restrictions necessitated by the rights and interests of the sovereignty of Portugal and the maintenance of public order, and so long as they are in harmony with international treaties and conventions.

ARTICLE 24: Religious missions overseas, being instruments of civilization and national influence, and establishments for the training of personnel for service in them and in the Portuguese *Padroado* shall possess a juridical character and shall be protected and assisted by the States as institutions of learning.

## Major Program of Movimento Popular de Libertação de Angola (MPLA) [2]

In this hour the concrete and immediate enemies of the Angolan people are the Portuguese colonialists and their agents, who will use all measures—violence, assassination, Machiavellism and subterfuge, military force, political and economic power, and cultural obscurantism—to maintain their sovereignty in Angola and to continue to oppress and exploit the Angolan people.

MPLA stands for the following program:

1. Immediate and Complete Independence: Liquidation in Angola by all available means of Portuguese colonial rule and all traces of colonialism and imperialism.

To fight in common with all the forces of Angolan patriots in a mass popular movement, in order that the Angolan people have the power to install in Angola a republican and democratic regime on the basis of total independence.

To abolish all the privileges which the colonial regime has conceded to the Portuguese nationals and to foreigners.

The sovereignty of the Angolan state must belong entirely and uniquely to the Angolan people without distinctions based on ethnic groups, class, age, political and religious beliefs.

The Angolan nation will have the sacred and inviolable right of self-determination whether in political, economic, diplomatic, military, and cultural planning or in any other sphere.

Revision of the Angolan position in all treaties, agreements and alliances which Portugal contracted without the free consent of the Angolan people.

A popular voluntary union with the purpose of liquidating whatever tendency of imperialistic aggression and all the acts and works which prejudice the independence, sovereignty, unity and territorial integrity of Angola.

The establishment of peace in Angola, based on a program of social justice, and the recognition by other nations of the independence, sovereignty, unity and territorial integrity of Angola.

2. National Unity: To guarantee equality to all ethnic groups in Angola and to reinforce their unity and to help bring about friendship among them.

Absolute prohibition of all tendencies to divide the Angolan nation.

To create conditions in Angola so that the thousands of Angolans who were forced to leave the country because of cruel treatment by the colonial regime would return to Angola.

Regions in which national minorities live in dense numbers and possess individual characters ought to become autonomous.

Each nationality or tribe will have the right to use and develop its own language—written and spoken—and to conserve or recreate its cultural heritage.

In the interest of the Angolan nation, economic and social solidarity must be instigated and developed as well as normal relations—in economic, social and cultural planning—between all the autonomous regions and all the nationalities or tribes in Angola.

Freedom of movement for all Angolan citizens which does not encroach upon national boundaries.

3. African Unity: Complete solidarity with all African peoples who are fighting for complete independence and against colonialism and imperialism, and in particular with the peoples and political movements which are fighting against Portuguese colonialism.

To work for the unity of all the peoples of the continent of Africa on the basis of respect for liberty, dignity and the right to develop their own political, economic and social systems.

Unity of all African countries based on popular will and expressed through democratic and peaceful means.

Opposition of any move to annex or to pressure one country over another.

In the process of uniting one or more African nations, it resists political, economic, social conquests upon the culture of the working class and the boundaries of each country.

4. Democratic Regime: Republican, democratic and secular government for Angola.

To guarantee freedom of speech, conscience, belief, press, assembly, associations, housing, correspondence, etc., for all the Angolan people.

All Angolan citizens—without distinction of nationality or tribe, of sex, social classification, cultural background, profession, wealth, religious belief or philosophical convictions—will have the right to vote at the age of eighteen years and the right to be elected after twenty-one years of age.

Elections will be based on universal suffrage, equal, direct and secret.

The Assembly of the Angolan nation will be the supreme legislative body of the State.

Members of the Assembly will be elected in free general elections. Legal political parties can present a common or separate list of their candidates.

The Assembly of Angola will formulate the first political constitution of the republic of Angola.

All members of the Assembly will have parliamentary immunity.

The Assembly will designate a coalition government which can effect a union among the various nationalities or tribes, social classes; and among the various political parties; and that the government will really express the will of the nation in favor of liberty and progress; and against political, economic, territorial or cultural alienation to the advantage of foreigners.

The government of the republic of Angola will be the supreme body and will exercise the executive power of the State. It will receive its power from the Assembly and will be responsible to that body.

Each autonomous region will have the right to adopt methods particularly suited to its conditions, but not contradictory to the general welfare of Angola.

Africanization of all administrative machinery of the country.

Guarantees of protection in accord with the Universal Declaration of Human Rights to all strangers who respect the laws in existence.

5. Economic Reconstruction and Plan of Production: Economic development through planning stages. Transformation of Angola into a country which is modern, prosperous, vigorous and economically and industrially independent.

Agricultural development, with long range planning, principally the abandoning of a one-crop system; increase in productivity and mechanization of agriculture.

Founding and progressive development of commercial and industrial enterprises, of consumers, wholesale, and producer's cooperatives. Progressive building of heavy and light industries; the latter for the production of consumer goods.

Exploration of the state of potential energy in the country.

Restoration and development of traditional African industries.

Abolition of economic privileges bestowed by the colonial regime upon Portuguese nationals and foreign commercial houses.

Development of communication and transport facilities.

Protection of industry and private enterprise.

Encouragement of industry and of private commerce which are useful to the State and life of the people.

Foreign economic enterprises must conform with the new laws of Angola. Protection of foreign economic activities which are useful to the progress and reinforcement of real independence of the Angolan people.

Development and vigorous activity of economic relations between cities and villages, with the idea of progressively improving rural conditions and the level of life of rural populations.

Effective implementation of a policy which considers, at the same time, the interests of employees and employers.

Establishment of a National Bank and currency. Avoidance of inflation and creation of a stable currency.

Control by the State for the best interest of all of foreign trade of Angola. Revision of the unfair agreement of Angola with Portugal. Combat the balance deficit of the commerce of Angola. A balancing of the books—of receipts and expenditures.

Abolition of the fiscal system introduced by Portuguese colonialists and creation of a new fiscal system; just, rational and simple.

Price control and prohibition of speculations.

6. Agrarian Reform: To introduce agrarian reform that will eliminate the existing injustices in relation to rural ownership; to liquidate

private monopoly of special rural production which is contrary to the denationalization of the Angolan soil; to fulfill the principle: the land is for those who till the soil.

Nationalization of land belonging to the enemy of the nationalist movement after immediate and complete independence of Angola; of traitors and proven enemies of the independent and democratic Angolan state.

Definition of the limits of private rural property, having in mind the rural situation of each locality. After revision of title on lands, the purchasing by the State, for a just price, lands which are owned beyond the limits established by law.

Distribution of land to those who do not have it and to those who have insufficient acreage. The beneficiaries of land legally distributed will not have to pay to the expropriators and to the State.

Protection of the right of conquest by farmers in the popular battle for an independent Angola.

7. Just Social Politics and of Progress: The State ought to protect the rights of workers and farmers, and of all social strata who have actively defended the independence of Angola; autonomy and unity of the Angolan people and territorial integrity of the country.

Immediate abolition of the regime of forced labor.

Respect for the independence of syndicates and legal organizations of workers.

An eight-hour day and progressive application of new laws for the protection of workers. The State will fix a minimum wage scale and will guard the rigorous application of the principle, "equal salary for equal work," without discrimination of sex, age and ethnic origin of workers.

Protection of churches, places and objects of worship of legal religious institutions.

In all planning—political, economic, social and cultural—women will have the same rights as men. Women and men are equal before the law.

State assistance to maternity patients and to infants.

Application of social assistance to all Angolan citizens deprived of means and victims of disease, or in situations of forced unemployment, or of old age or infirmity.

Solution for unemployment. Work security for artisans, workers, functionaries and for youths who complete their studies.

Assistance to all citizens who are disabled because of active participation in combat for the independence of Angola. Assistance to families whose members died for the liberation of the Angolan nation.

8. Development of Instruction, Culture and Education: Prohibition of colonial and imperialistic culture and education. Reform of instruction in actual practice. Development of instruction, culture and education in the service of liberty and of peaceful progress of the Angolan people.

To combat vigorously and rapidly illiteracy throughout the country. Public instruction will become the obligation of the State and will be under its direction.

To progressively establish compulsory and free primary education. To develop secondary technical-professional schools and to establish higher education.

Establishment of cultural relations with foreign countries. Formation and perfection of technical units necessary to the building up of the nation. To give impetus to the study of the sciences, technology, letters and arts.

To institute in rural areas, efficient and adequate medical and sanitary aid for rural populations. Equal development on a national scale of medical and sanitary assistance.

Elimination of prostitution and alcoholism.

Stimulation and support of progressive youth activities. To support and protect, throughout the country, physical culture.

9. National Defense: Establishment of an army for national defense, with sufficient power, intimately linked with the people and commanded wholly by Angolan citizens.

To arm, equip and unqualifiedly train an army. To install and unify new military and political instruction for the army. To establish democratic relations between officers and enlisted men. To consolidate discipline. Within the army to develop and create a national conscience, and to combat all regional tendencies.

Prohibition of foreign military bases on the national territory.

10. Independent and Peaceful Foreign Relations: To establish and maintain diplomatic relations with all the countries of the world on the basis of the following principles: mutual respect of national sovereignty and territorial integrity; nonaggression; noninterference in internal matters; equal and reciprocal advantages; peaceful coexistence.

Respect for the Charter of the United Nations.

Nonalignment to whatever military bloc.

Special relations with our good neighbors and collaboration with the surrounding nations of Angola.

Protection of Angolan residents in foreign countries.

## Minimum Program of the MPLA

1. Urgent formation of a solid Angolan front for freedom, which will bring together in a larger union, all political parties, all popular organizations, all armed forces, all prominent personalities of the country, all religious organizations, all nationalities or tribes of Angola, all African social classes, all Angolan residents in foreign countries, without distinction of political leanings, of wealth, sex, age; the aim to be:

2. Fighting, by all means, in the liquidation in Angola of colonial Portuguese domination and all vestiges of colonialism and imperialism, and for the immediate and complete independence of the Angolan nation.

3. To defend constantly, in the first place, the interest of the mass farmers and workers, the two groups most important to the country and who constitute jointly almost all the population of Angola.

4. Alliance with all progressive forces of the world; the conquest of sympathy and support of all peoples in the cause of freedom for the Angolan people.

## Declaration of the Steering Committee of União das Populações de Angola (UPA)

The Union of the Populations of Angola, conscious of its responsibility and the rights of the peoples of Angola, declares that it is devoted in its activities to the realization and acquisition of the immediate independence of the people, moreover to its acquisition by pacific and democratic means. It will spare itself no sacrifice. In consequence:

Peasants, Unemployed, Forced Laborers, your duty is clear. You are the most downtrodden. It is you who suffer most from colonial oppression. That is why you have the greatest interest in the re-establishment of the Angolan nation. For the past five centuries your ancestors, your parents and you, yourselves, have been condemned to exert all your efforts for the enrichment of only the Portuguese colonialists. You create the riches but you have not the right to profit from them. Your sweat is the grease of the colonist; your blood is sucked by the colonial vampire, and you are left to languish in misery and humiliation.

The Union of the Populations of Angola formally pledges to bring an end to this mortal sickness of the territory of Angola. It calls on you all to contribute to the liquidation of Portuguese colonialism in the national territory of Angola.

*Women.* The women of Ghana, Guinea, Cameroons, Togo, Congo and Somaliland all participated in the heroic combat against colonialism. The hour is past when the women remained at their firesides and were mere spectators of events. Your husbands are not paid, your children are not fed or given schooling; they serve only as machines to permit the colonists to live an increasingly easy life at the cost of the misery of the peoples of Angola. You have the same rights as the men. The Union of the Populations of Angola is determined to establish a democratic regime which will, without distinction of sex, permit each individual to develop his personality and contribute to the development and productivity of the Angolan nation.

Most of the time now you are requisitioned and forced to work on forced labor projects. The pitiless colonialist beast requires of you the most inhuman and vile labor. The Union of the Populations of Angola considers that this scandal has lasted too long already, that the hour has struck when you should have a respectable and dignified lot in life. Wherever you are: organize, prepare to take up and spread the orders of the Union of the Populations of Angola.

Erase fear and submission from your lives. You must prove to the occupying power that you are conscious of the justice of your cause.

*Tribal Chiefs.* Certainly your position is difficult. For a long time you have unknowingly served the colonialist interests and permitted the exploitation of the people. Although your mission as chiefs was to protect and serve the people of Angola. Certain members of your group have become instruments of colonialism. They have permitted the recruitment of forced laborers and have supported the policy of heavy taxation, and in a great portion of Angola their position has made them traitors.

The Union of the Populations of Angola is not ignorant of the terrible pressures you have suffered from colonialism, but it knows also that at this time, when a great movement is shaking Africa, you must not stand idly by. You must fully realize that the moment has come for you to make your choice between your country, your sons, your brothers on the one hand, and the colonists on the other. That is why we ask you to think carefully.

During the year 1960, all the African peoples are to unite their efforts for the eviction of colonialism from Africa. The African peoples and the people of Angola will be pitiless for the men who have not been able to choose the side of justice and truth. From today onward, the people are judging you. All that you do against the people will be held against you. This is no longer the time when a chief could be ordered by a European and blindly strike and punish his subjects at any moment and under any circumstances. The end of the arbitrary has come. You must understand.

*Youth.* You are the seeds of Angola, it is toward you that we all turn our hopes and our concerns. It is to you that we all look for new values, values which will bring Angola's voice to be heard immediately in the concert of nations.

You must develop your national conscience and your human conscience. You must erase from your soul all traces of inferiority complex. You must no longer permit yourselves to be beaten down; you must take in your hands the destiny of your land and of your people. And you must stand ready as the determined reserves to come to the aid of your elder brothers who are so enthusiastically setting in motion the battle for national liberation.

*Portuguese Colonists.* The Union of the Populations of Angola is not the enemy of the Portuguese but it is against a system of spoliation which robs our land of all existence as a nation and which condemns 4,500,000 inhabitants to illiteracy, humiliation and famine. The Union of the Populations of Angola is fighting with all its force against this system. It begs you not to stand in opposition to the advance of history.

Certain of your members have established colossal fortunes on the backs of the Angolans. They must be made to understand that the hour has come when they must make restitution to the Angolans for their land and their resources.

As for the others, the Union of the Populations of Angola tells them that they may remain in Angola in new found peace so that together we can work for the establishment of an Angolan Republic, democratic and socially just.

*Portuguese People.* You know, you are not ignorant of the lamentable state in which the people of Angola find themselves. Colonists who have come from Portugal, supported by the Army and a pitiless administration, have brought an unbelievable reign of terror to a population of 4,500,000 people.

The Union of the Populations of Angola calls upon all the democrats, workers, Christians and men of good faith of Portugal to unite their efforts to work against this disgrace to the twentieth century, which dishonors and disgraces the name of Portugal.

*Portuguese State.* The regime that the Union of the Populations of Angola will establish in Angola will be democratic. It will be democratic because the power will be exercised by the people for the people. It will be socially just because it will be exercised directly and specifically by the most needy masses. The lands will be distributed to those who work them.

The Union of the Populations of Angola will abolish all the special privileges and exceptions established by your representatives. The women will also have the right of vote.

Privileges will be abolished, each person shall have an equal right to education. Unemployment will be declared a national emergency and every force will erase this situation.

Every man and every woman inhabitant in Angola, regardless of nationality, race or religion, will have the same rights as individuals, and the same rights will be respected in relation to their belongings.

The emancipating movement of the colonial peoples is strongly developed. It has acquired extraordinary power in numbers and today is irresistible.

Men who refuse to recognize and take into consideration the prodigious wave of independence which is sweeping the world are unrealistic and irresponsible.

The people of Africa, from Algeria to the Cape, have come to their feet with the cry and the warning: "Africa for the Africans."

The Union of the Populations of Angola is certain that you will fulfill your responsibilities. As for ourselves, we have already undertaken our own, and any resistance to the movement is destined to be a total failure.

*African Peoples.* Our continent, which is in the shape of an interrogation point, has in its heart the destiny of all present day mankind. For so long in bondage, it is commencing to make its voice heard in the concert of nations. No African can remain indifferent to the existence of colonialism on our continent. Each one of us has a definite duty to perform: to liquidate the colonial regime, the colonialist spirit, the colonial ideal, and to establish democracy in Africa, to construct the United States of Africa on the foundation of the autonomy of the democratic units which will compose it.

Taking into consideration the resolutions adopted at the Congresses of Bandung, Cairo, Accra, Tunis and Conakry, and taking into account the watchwords of Liberty, Independence and Action in Africa, the

Union of the Populations of Angola is determined to join the African Anti-Colonialist Front and to join battle against Portuguese colonialism and continue the fight to total victory. It expects all the Independent African States to aid and support its movement unconditionally. It expects all men, all women, to give their full support for a free Africa as the common undertaking of the 200,000,000 souls who make up the population of this great continent.

*International Opinion.* The Union of the Populations of Angola pledges itself to spare no effort in bringing the occupying power which controls the human and economic interests of the Portuguese to a pacific solution.

Are not the people of Angola essentially a peace-loving people?

In spite of repression, torture, oppression, exploitation, humiliation, in spite of slavery, the Angolan people have always given proof of absolute pacifism, not out of moral weakness, but because of their firm belief that between men there is always the possibility of pacific solution to any problem. And today it is time for the Portuguese to respond to this call.

The Union of the Populations of Angola calls the world to be its witness.

The solidly entrenched camp of colonialism which is Angola today is a disgrace to all of humanity. It is the duty of every man worthy of the name to participate in the restoration of human dignity in Angola.

The Union of the Populations of Angola calls upon all international organizations and bodies, for them to bring pressure on Portugal so that the regime of exploitation and willful genocide in Angola shall cease, and that the territory shall recover its independence of ancient days.

# United Nations Declaration on the Granting of Independence to Colonial Countries and Peoples

1. The subjection of peoples to alien subjugation, domination and exploitation constitutes a denial of fundamental human rights, is contrary to the Charter of the United Nations and is an impediment to the promotion of world peace and cooperation.

2. All peoples have the right to self-determination; by virtue of that

right they freely determine their political status and freely pursue their economic, social and cultural development.

3. Inadequacy of political, economic, social or educational preparedness should never serve as a pretext for delaying independence.

4. All armed action or repressive measures of all kinds directed against dependent peoples shall cease in order to enable them to exercise peacefully and freely their right to complete independence, and the integrity of their national territory shall be respected.

5. Immediate steps shall be taken, in trust and non-self-governing territories or all other territories which have not yet attained independence, to transfer all powers to the peoples of those territories, without any conditions or reservations, in accordance with their freely expressed will and desire, without any distinction as to race, creed, or color, in order to enable them to enjoy complete independence and freedom.

6. Any attempt aimed at the partial or total disruption of the national unity and the territorial integrity of a country is incompatible with the purposes and principles of the Charter of the United Nations.

7. All states shall observe faithfully and strictly the provisions of the Charter of the United Nations, the Universal Declaration of Human Rights and the present declaration on the basis of equality, noninterference in the internal affairs of all states and respect for the sovereign rights of all peoples and their territorial integrity.

# APPENDIX II. RELIGIOUS SOCIETIES

## Roman Catholic

1482 Diogo Cão discovers the Congo.

1490-1491 Embassy sent to king of Congo with representatives of the Franciscan mission.

1548 Jesuit mission established at São Salvador.

1552 Jesuits abandon mission at São Salvador.

1575 Luanda founded by Dias de Novães and Jesuits.

1614 Return of Jesuits to São Salvador.

1600 Formation of a Jesuit college. Entrance of Tertiaries of St. Francis with responsibility in educational work.

1640-1648 Dutch occupation of Luanda and curtailment of religious activity.

1650-1651 Capuchins begin their work in Luanda.

1716 Bishopric officially transferred to Luanda.

1800 African clergy assuming active role in parish activities.

1865 Entrance of French fathers of the Order of the Holy Ghost.

1875 Secular priests from Sernache do Bonjardin stationed as parish priests.

1881 Re-establishment of São Salvador mission by Father António Barroso.

1881 Sisters of St. Joseph of Cluny arrive in Luanda to assist in health and educational programs.

1926 Mission activity greatly increased with the coming of the "New State" under the Salazar regime.

## Protestants

1878 English Baptist Missionary Society. Their work is concentrated in Portuguese Congo.

1880 The American Board of Commissioners for Foreign Missions. They represent the Congregational Christian Churches of the U.S.A. Their work is in central Angola.

1884 The Methodist Episcopal Church. Bishop William Taylor and a party of missionaries from America began this work among the Kimbundu-speaking people, making Luanda their first port of entry.

1897 The Angola Evangelical Mission. It was founded by the Rev. M. Z. Stober and has an undenominational basis supported by many friends in England, Scotland and Wales. They concentrated their work among the Kikongo-speaking Africans in northern Angola.

1897 Mission Philafricaine. This society may be called a by-product of Bishop Taylor's mission. Heli Chatelain, the founder of this mission, Swiss by birth but a naturalized American citizen, went out with Taylor in the capacity of linguist. In 1897, Chatelain established at Caluquembe, in the south of Angola, an independent mission station, supported mainly by friends in Switzerland.

1910 Christian and Missionary Alliance. Their work has been in the Cabinda district on the enclave of the Congo River. The work has now been taken over by the Canadian Baptist Missionary Society.

1914 South Africa General Mission. In 1914 the Rev. A. W. Bailey crossed over from Northern Rhodesia into Southern Angola to begin work in this vast untouched area. The year 1920 brought workers from the United States and Canada to bolster the meager missionary staff. The multitribal units increased the obstacles in the building of a united Christian community.

1925 North Angola Mission. This is a very small mission located in the coffee country of northern Angola.

1927 United Church of Canada. They continue to carry on the

cooperative work begun by the former Congregational Church of the present United Church.

1950 Assemblies of God. Their principal area of work has been in the Gabela and Novo Redondo region. Because of the activities of the white Portuguese missionaries, the state closed the mission and expelled them from the area.

1954 Canadian Baptist Missionary Society. They have taken over the former Stober mission and the work in Cabinda formerly supervised by the Christian Missionary Alliance.

# NOTES

## Introduction

1. *Time* magazine, February 17, 1961.

2. *New York Times*, February 6, 1961.

3. Hodgkin, Thomas, *Nationalism in Colonial Africa*, New York University Press, New York, 1957, p. 23.

It is difficult to understand nationalism and politics in Africa by wholly defining the common properties of political systems. The rise of trade unionism, the forming of Christian Separatist groups, are common features in the dominant theme of the reaction against "colonial imperialism." Coleman's approach inclines to give a fragmentary view of the rise of African politics.

The Africa of the past on which the present is built does not separate the economic, the religious, the political self. Religious symbols and rituals are often dominant aspects within a political party. Furthermore the study of politics in Africa cannot be dissociated from the history of the people. The implications are the following: first, that African history did not begin with the European invasion; second, the dynamics of change within the present situation existed in the pre-European society; third, pre-European dynamics still have influence in the political situation today; and fourth, present African leaders are using this pre-European history to maintain their positions.

4. *Ibid.*, p. 23.

5. *Ibid.*, p. 25.

## I. The Setting

1. Duffy, James, *Portuguese Africa*, Harvard University Press, Cambridge, 1959, p. 50.

2. *Angola*, Portuguese Province in Africa, Angola Institute Edition, Luanda, 1953, p. 36.

3. *Ibid.*, pp. 125-126.

4. *Anuário Estatístico de Angola*, 1956, Luanda, p. 19.

5. Ennis, Merlin W., "The Angola Mission," unpublished typescript, Boston, 1956.

6. Childs, Gladwyn, *Umbundu Kinship and Character*, Oxford Uni-

versity Press, London, 1949, pp. 170-171.

7. Nordby, Juel A., "Political Roles Among the Kimbundu," unpublished typescript, Boston, 1960.

8. Childs, Gladwyn, op. cit., p. 22.

9. Ibid., p. 21.

10. Ibid., p. 25.

11. Ibid., p. 181.

12. Delgado, Ralph, Ao Sul do Cuanza, vol. 1, Lisboa, 1944, p. 388.

13. Missionary Herald, 1886, The American Board, Boston, p. 228.

14. Delgado, op. cit., pp. 393-394.

15. Ibid.

16. Ibid., vol. II, p. 301.

17. Ibid., p. 304.

18. Ibid., p. 305.

19. Ibid., pp. 604-606.

20. Ibid., pp. 607-609.

21. Couçeiro, Henrique da Paiva, Angola—Dois Anos de Governo Junho 1907—Junho 1909, Editora a Nacional, Lisboa, p. 62.

22. Ibid.

23. Delgado, op. cit., pp. 270-271.

24. Anuário Estatístico de Angola, 1956, Luanda, p. 21.

## II. Portugal's Colonial Policy

1. General Act of Berlin Conference, Article XXXIV, February 26, 1885.

2. Caetano, Marcello, Portugal e o Direito Colonial Internacional, Lisboa, 1948, pp. 15-16.

3. Duffy, James, Portuguese Africa, p. 270.

4. I was in Luanda when the demonstrations took place at the Governor's Palace.

5. The World Book Encyclopedia, vol. 13 (1955 ed.), Field Enterprises, Inc., Chicago, pp. 6515-6517.

6. Camoens, The Lusiads, trans. William C. Atkinson, Penguin Classics, 1952, p. 236.

7. Duffy, op. cit., p. 295.

8. North American Assembly on African Affairs, Wittenberg College, Springfield, Ohio, June 16-25, 1952.

9. Ministério das Colónias, Secretaria Geral, Decreto No. 18:570, 8 de Julho de 1930, Acto Colonial, tit. II, Dos Indígenas (see appendix for document).

10. Ibid., Art. 22.

11. Davidson, Basil, The African Awakening, Macmillan, New York, 1955, p. 205.

12. Ibid., p. 202.

13. Angola, Portuguese Province in Africa, pp. 105-106.

14. Hodgkin, Thomas, Nationalism in Colonial Africa, pp. 11-12.

15. Duffy, op. cit., p. 280.

16. Angola, Portuguese Province in Africa, pp. 195-196.

17. Ibid., p. 100.

18. Ibid., p. 39.

19. Deutsch, Karl W., "Toward an Inventory of Basic Trends and Patterns in Comparative and International Products," American Political Science Review, March 1960, vol. LIV, p. 56.

20. London Times, June 3, 1960.

21. I gathered this information while on a trip through this area in September 1959.

22. Lupi, Luis C., Portugal in Africa. The Significance of the Visits

of the President of the Republic to the Overseas Provinces, Agência Geral do Ultramar, 1957, pp. 8-9.
23. *Anuário Estatístico de Angola*, 1958, Luanda, as quoted in the *Portuguese and Colonial Bulletin*,

London, vol. 1, no. 1, February 1961.
24. *Anuário Estatístico*, 1959.
25. *O Planalto*, Nova Lisboa, Angola, August 29, 1961.

## III. Disruptive Sources

1. *Angola*, Portuguese Province in Africa, p. 63.
2. *Anuário Estatístico de Angola*, 1956, Luanda, p. 73.
3. Decreto No. 18:578 (see appendix for document).
4. Rego, Silva, *Curso de Missionologia*, Agência Geral do Ultramar, Lisboa, 1956, p. 289.
5. Tucker, John T., *Angola, The Land of the Blacksmith Prince*, World Dominion Press, London, 1933, p. 49.
6. *Anuário Etatístico de Angola*, 1956, Luanda, p. 73.
7. *Ibid.*, 1954, pp. 158-185; 1956, p. 73.
8. Decreto No. 77, Boletim Oficial, Luanda, 17 de Dezembro de 1921, lo serie No. 50.
9. *Angola, op. cit.*, p. 64.
10. *Anuário Estatístico*, 1956, Luanda, pp. 73-80.
11. *Ibid.*
12. Mason, Philip, *Year of Decision*, Rhodesia and Nyasaland 1960, Oxford University Press, London, 1960, p. 265.

13. *Ibid.*
14. *Anuário Estatístico de Angola*, 1956, Luanda, p. 38.
15. *Ibid.*, p. 42.
16. *Ibid.*, p. 177.
17. *Ibid.*, p. 186.
18. *Ibid.*, p. 167.
19. Karefa-Smart, John and Rena, *The Halting Kingdom*, Friendship Press, 1959, p. 26.
20. Tucker, *op. cit.*, p. 14.
21. Rego, *op. cit.*, p. 284.
22. *Ibid.*, p. 299.
23. Berlin Act, Art. VI (see appendix for document).
24. *Anuário Estatístico de Angola*, 1950, Luanda.
25. Childs, Gladwyn, *Umbundu Kinship and Character*, p. 223.
26. Tucker, *op. cit.*, pp. 109-111.
27. Hodgkin, Thomas, *Nationalism in Colonial Africa*, pp. 94-95.
28. Schachter, Ruth, "A Note on the Classification of Political Parties in French Speaking West Africa," unpublished typescript, Boston, 1959.

## IV. Angolan Nationalist Groups

1. *Portuguese and Colonial Bulletin*, London, vol. 1, no. 1, February, 1961.
2. *Angola*, Portuguese Province in Africa, p. 191.

3. Pinto, Ferreira, *Angola*, Lisboa, 1926, pp. 522-524.
4. *Portuguese and Colonial Bulletin*, supplement to no. 1, February 1961.

5. Du Bois, William Edward, *The World and Africa*, Viking Press, New York, 1947, p. 241.

6. *Ibid.*

7. *Estatística Industrial*, 1958, Lisbon, Instituto Nacional de Estatísticas, 1959, as quoted in *Portuguese and Colonial Bulletin*, vol. 1, no. 1, February 1961.

8. Deutsch, Karl W., "Toward an Inventory of Basic Trends and Patterns in Comparative and International Products," pp. 34-57.

9. Declaration of the Steering Committee of União das Populações de Angola, Leopoldville, pp. 13-14.

10. *Ibid.*, p. 17.

11. *Anuário Estatístico de Angola*, 1956, Luanda, p. 297.

12. *O Planalto*, Nova Lisboa, March 1960.

13. London *Times*, May 27, 1960.

14. *Anuário Estatístico de Angola*, 1956, Luanda, p. 96.

15. *Portuguese and Colonial Bulletin*, London, vol. 1, no. 1, February 1961, p. 3.

16. *Anuário Estatístico de Angola*, 1956, p. 297.

# V. Portugal Under Fire

1. Department of State *Bulletin*, July 11, 1949, Washington, D.C.

2. Carvalho, de Martins, *Coloquios de Política Internacional*, "O Colonialism e a ONU," Estudos de Ciências Políticas e Sociais III, Ministro de Ultramar, Lisboa, 1957, pp. 28-29.

3. United Nations Charter, Chap. XI, Art. 73, Sec. (e).

4. *United Nations Review*, New York, December 1960, p. 19.

5. *Ibid.*, p. 19.

6. *Ibid.*, p. 20.

7. *Ibid.*

8. *Ibid.*, p. 21.

9. *Ibid.*, p. 22.

10. *O Planalto*, Nova Lisboa, October 21, 1960.

11. *New York Times*, December 11, 1960.

12. *O Planalto*, November 11, 1960.

13. *United Nations Review*, New York, December 1960, p. 21.

14. *Ibid.*, p. 21.

15. *Ibid.*

16. Department of State *Bulletin*, Washington, D.C., June 6, 1960.

17. *New York Times*, January 11, 1961.

18. *Ibid.*, January 27, 1961.

19. *Christian Science Monitor*, Boston, February 3, 1961.

20. *New York Times*, February 11, 1961.

21. *Ibid.*, March 15, 1961.

22. *Ibid.*, March 17, 1961.

## VI. The Outbreak of Violence in Angola

1. *O Comercio*, April 12, 1961, Luanda, Angola.
2. *Christian Science Monitor*, May 3, 1961, Boston, Mass.
3. *Ibid.*, May 12, 1961, Boston.
4. *New York Times*, March 30, 1961, New York.
5. *Ibid.*
6. *Ibid.*, May 10, 1961, New York.
7. *Ibid.*, May 3, 1961, New York.
8. The *Star*, April 29, 1961, Johannesburg, Union of South Africa.
9. *Christian Science Monitor*, April 5, 1961, Boston, Mass.
10. Manifesto by African nationalists distributed in January 1961.

## VII. What of the Future?

1. Hance, William A., and Van Dongen, Irene S., "The Port of Lobito and the Benguela Railway," *Geographical Review*, vol. XLVI, no. 4, 1956, p. 466.
2. *New York Times*, March 20, 1961.
3. *Ibid.*
4. *United Nations Review*, New York, January 1961, p. 40.
5. Djassi, Abel, *The Facts About Portugal's African Colonies*, Union of Democratic Publication, London, p. 20.
6. Hodgkin, Thomas, *Nationalism in Colonial Africa*, p. 190.
7. *New York Times*, February 11, 1961.

## Appendix I

1. Tucker, John T., *Angola*, pp. 163-165.
2. Translated by the author.

# INDEX